LEADERS
CREATE
SPACE

Transform Disruption into
Clarity for Life and Work

Steve Laswell

Published by Best Seller Publishing®, Pasadena, CA

Best Seller Publishing® is a registered trademark

Printed in the United States of America.

ISBN 978-1-946978-65-3

This publication is designed to provide accurate and authoritative information with regard to the subject matter covered. It is sold with the understanding that the publisher is not engaged in rendering legal, accounting, or other professional advice. If legal advice or other expert assistance is required, the services of a competent professional should be sought. The opinions expressed by the authors in this book are not endorsed by Best Seller Publishing® and are the sole responsibility of the author rendering the opinion.

Most Best Seller Publishing® titles are available at special quantity discounts for bulk purchases for sales promotions, premiums, fundraising, and educational use. Special versions or book excerpts can also be created to fit specific needs.

For more information, please write:

Best Seller Publishing®

1346 Walnut Street, #205

Pasadena, CA 91106

or call 1(626) 765 9750

Toll Free: 1(844) 850-3500

Visit us online at: www.BestSellerPublishing.org

Table of Contents

The Secret to Engaging People

Introduction

Imagine we reconnect at a networking event when I ask, "How are you?" Quick, what's your answer? "I'm so___." Fill in the blank. More often than not, the answer to that question is, "I'm so busy." It seems to me that every morning people in the workplace are required to pick up their badge that says "I'm so BUSY." We wear it with pride. We pin it on and we wear it throughout the day and we polish it as necessary. We wear it until everyone else is gone before we lay the Busy Badge back on our desk as we go home. "I'm so busy."

Try it sometime. Leave the office on time and say, "I'm going home." "I'm going to the gym." Look at the faces of those left behind; likely, your credibility is at stake because you're leaving "on time." Meanwhile, everyone shines their "I'm so busy" badge again.

Why? It's become normal, maybe even the *new normal*. It's the usual or the expected to be so busy. It occurs so naturally. We don't have to work at being busy; we just are busy. We stay busy. We feel good when we're busy. The whirlwind calls our name. We love it. We feel so good about ourselves when we're so busy.

The problem with the new normal is that it produces the average. It creates the unexceptional, the unremarkable. Then there is the matter of conformity. You begin to do what other people do. You begin to behave in a way that is acceptable to most people. You begin to act in accordance with prevailing standards, and suddenly you're "so busy," too. Yes, it's easy to conform, to accept what's become normal. It's easy to settle for less than what is possible. It's easy to settle for status quo behavior and low performance. It's easy to feel the pain of being stuck or frustrated, while accepting it as "that's just life."

In the busy life, it's easy to live an average life, to be unexceptional, to conform to a world around us. In the busy life, it's easy to be selfish or lazy. It's easy to eat poorly, to be inactive, to not read a book. In the busy life, it's easy to be controlling and reactive and disengaged. In the busy life, it's easy to accept the chaos, the distractions, the exhaustion, the status quo life. It's easy to have habits, behaviors, and thinking that hold you captive in what is called a *comfort zone*, but it's anything but. Jim Collins says it well when he writes, "Few people attain great lives, in large part, because it's so *easy to settle* for a good life."

Beyond the comfort zone lies a safety zone. In simple terms, it's when you see the risk, but you go for it. Instead of hesitating when you know what to do, you go for it. You take action. It's where the risk of staying is overshadowed by the risk of moving, and you act.

The line represents "unproductive behavior." It's the stuff that holds you back from your full potential from expanding your influence with

THE THREE ZONES OF "HERE" TO "THERE" JOURNEY

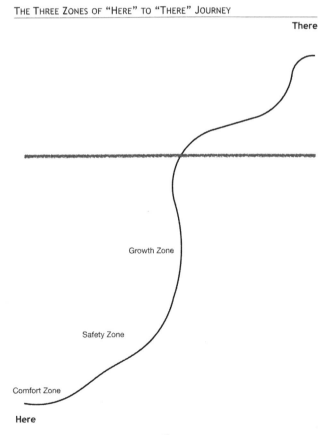

others. It could be a habit, a belief or way of thinking that restricts instead of liberates. It could represent micro-management, poor decision making, ineffective communication. The line represents where a breakthrough is required to get "There."

Outside of the safety zone is the growth zone. This is where you and I engage in a *process of change*. This is where you exercise your ability and willingness to learn and change. The key word in the growth zone is transformation. Yes, transformation is about change. It is to become different in order to do different. It is to become someone better. It is about changing from the inside out. What is it that's required to experience such transformation? To move from good enough to my best self? It is to **create space**.

Leaders create space, and by that I mean *the disciplined use of time, place, and resources to reflect on truth in the Story*. To conform is easy. To be transformed, to change behavior is hard work. It's intentional. It requires a renewing of the mind, a change of thinking. It may require new tools and new habits to help us go from where we are today to where we want to be in the future. What is the enemy of creating space as a leader? That's right—it's being busy. It's all the noise and distractions. It's the devices. It's no time to think, no margin to listen. You could call it insanity when you keep doing the same thing over and over again, hoping to get a different result. In the pages that follow, I will be your Sherpa—a guide on the adventure to reach new heights of personal and professional growth. I will show you how to create space to move from here (which we can celebrate) to there (which is better).

This book is for you if you want to accelerate your personal growth. If you want a framework to sustain your leadership development. If you want to develop your core skills, your people skills. If you want to exercise your ability to change behavior and improve your performance to have positive influence in the lives of others. If you want to reduce unnecessary stress and conflict. If you want a battle plan to produce breakthrough performance. Come, join me on this adventure. And as we take the journey together, it is my hope that you will help other people make their journey, too. As my friend, Todd Craig, says, "If we are to have lives of significance, we must become significantly different."

It's the Next Level Journey from Here to There. What we'll find is that to experience true transformation and change requires an intentional interruption of doing in order to think and of slowing down to accelerate our development as leaders.

Leaders Create Space; come join me.

Part One:

Write the Story You Want to Tell

Chapter One
The People Project

Beautiful people do not just happen.
—Elisabeth Kübler-Ross

As I take my seat on the airplane, I'm relaxed and approachable. Sizing up my seatmate, I take on the challenge to engage him in a conversation.

"Where are you headed?"

"I'm going to Denver."

Undeterred by the short answer, I continue, "Oh really, what takes you to Denver, business or pleasure?"

"Business. I'm visiting one of our field offices. We've got some issues I've got to resolve."

"What's your role with the company?"

"I'm vice president of operations. What do you do?" he asks me.

"I'm an executive coach. I help develop self-managed teams and leaders."

"That must be interesting." Terry—the former stranger in seat 12A—seems to relax, which opens the door for me to ask more questions, as he continues telling me his story.

Truly curious, I ask, "What's your biggest challenge?"

"We recently promoted someone to run the Denver field operations. The transition has been more turbulent than we anticipated. She knows the business and has performed really well. She rose through the ranks, but feedback indicates she has weak communication skills and is a bit too controlling. A few of our top performers are frustrated. Her behavior is getting in the way of her successful transition."

How many times have I heard some variation of the same story, as a leadership development coach?

Nine Observations Regarding Business and People

Over the years, I've made a list of my observations about business and people.

NUMBER ONE: **The business of business is people.** When I first entered the radio industry as a rookie account manager for Clear Channel in Oklahoma City, I was out of my comfort zone. For me, it was a brand-new career in a brand-new industry. A year-and-a-half later, I was promoted to General Sales Manager of the number-one billing station in Oklahoma City.

A couple of years later, another company, Cox Radio, recruited me to another market. With that company, I went through an executive leadership program and earned another promotion. I had a ten-year, fast-track journey through radio.

When people asked, "How did that happen?" I would always say that, to me, the business of business is people, and radio was just a storefront. Yes, I had to have some technical expertise and prove I could do the job, but the reason I succeeded was because I understood that the business of business is people.

NUMBER TWO: **Business eats people.** This is not a slam on business. Business takes raw material and it produces something, then exports it and is immediately hungry for more. That's great with raw material, but we're talking about people and their lives.

"Business eats people" means that as the leader of my own life, I have to set boundaries, create margin, and decide how much I'm going to feed the beast. Otherwise, the beast will take it all. As the leader of a department or a team or a company, there is a responsibility to ensure that my business plan and the expectations I have regarding my employees are reasonable and allow work-life balance—life-harmony, if you will.

NUMBER THREE: **People don't think.** Remember the last time that you did something that was kind of stupid, or unintelligent. After the situation was over, and you were telling the story, did you think, "Well, I didn't think that would happen"? What about when an employee comes into your office and explains that he has done something unwise, and when you confront him about the situation, he replies, "Well, I didn't think that would happen"? The reality is we do the *unthinkable* when we don't create space to think.

NUMBER FOUR: **People need help to become successful people.** What do people want? How do they achieve it? When I talk to successful people and hear their stories, I find most are humble and quick to acknowledge the influence of others. As we'll discover later in the book, most people want help getting better.

NUMBER FIVE: **It takes mature people to develop mature people.** How much immature behavior do you witness in your work place? How much dysfunction have you witnessed in the work place, perhaps even on your team? If we're going to have mature employees and teams it is going to take mature people, and that starts with us.

NUMBER SIX: **Take care of the people, and the people will take care of the business.** Research supports that even the millennials are looking for companies that will help them to develop. To them, work is about more than a paycheck, more than money. It's about the opportunity to grow, to improve their performance, and to make a contribution to a winning team.

NUMBER SEVEN: **If you take care of the people, and they don't take care of the business, they're not your people.** There are several challenges here that require soul searching as a leader. Questions regarding a good fit, onboarding, and training; clear job descriptions and expectations; coaching and development to support success. Did we set this person up for success?

NUMBER EIGHT: **It's supposed to be hard.** I remember watching an NBA game when Kevin Durant still played for the Oklahoma City

Thunder. Durant had just been called for another foul. Now, if you aren't an NBA fan, you may not know that the majority of "calls" are met with shock, protest, laughter, disbelief, running away from the scene, gestures, and occasionally, acceptance. Durant was frustrated with the call. During the shooting of the free throws, he wandered over to the score table, where Coach Billy Donovan addressed him with a smirk, "Kevin, it's supposed to be hard." Winning in business, when the business of business is people, is hard.

And finally, NUMBER NINE: **Everyone wants to be appreciated.**

The Journey

I think about life as a Journey. It is about traveling from one place to another. Traveling is about going from "Here" to "There," from one level of success to another, from one level of influence to another, from one level of maturity to another.

When I work with successful people or I speak to audiences, I get a chuckle every time I ask, "How many of you can identify with, 'I got here in spite of myself'?" Yes, we're all in better places than we may have expected, or certainly planned, when we were in our graduation ceremonies, back in the day.

The Here-to-There Journey is more about the leader I am becoming than the ladder I'm climbing. The Journey relates to our growing as human beings and becoming more mature people who have personal influence with others. In fact, this Journey requires you to slow down to accelerate the development. The Here-to-There Journey is the Story that you are writing, right now.

One Lifetime, So Many Stories

When it comes to the Story, there is your Story, my Story, and our Story. The Story connects us. We'll soon discover truth is in the Story; it teaches us where we need to change or get better, what holds us back. This is the power of Story. Here are five realities about the Story.

REALITY NUMBER ONE: **Everyone has a Story.** Whether you are in your office as you read this or in your favorite reading nook, think of the people in your life. Everywhere you look, whether it's in the office, at home, or in the grocery store, everywhere, there is another set of eyes, there is a Story.

Wouldn't it be interesting if we knew one another's Stories? Because, it matters how we got Here, where we are today. *Everyone has a Story.*

REALITY NUMBER TWO: **Every day we add to our Story.** Some days, life is so simple that we add just a sentence or two. Some days, it feels as though we've written a few paragraphs. Other days are chapter changers—there is such a big change that it feels like a new chapter in our life. Then there are those times where the change is so dramatic that it feels like we started writing a whole new volume of our Story.

REALITY NUMBER THREE: **Today, you will have influence on someone's Story.** Positive or not, you have already influenced someone today by the way you presented yourself, your manner of greeting , your body language, the questions you asked, the posture you took, and your ability to listen. You have influence every day on the lives of other people and their Stories.

REALITY NUMBER FOUR: **There's always more to the Story.** I love to remember this because it helps me challenge my assumptions: If we remember that there is more to someone's Story, it slows us down in our judgments of one another, and it helps us not jump to conclusions.

When someone comes into your office or enters the team meeting, remember there's always more to the Story that could explain the way they are showing up today. Basically, it's about giving grace to others in the same way we'd like to have grace given to us.

REALITY NUMBER FIVE: **You are responsible to write your Story.** Sometimes in our early lives, people say things that get stuck in our minds and in our memories. It may have been a school teacher who said, "you'll never be a writer," or it may have been a parent who said something that cut to the quick and lodged in your memory. The challenge for us, as we go through life, is to take the responsibility to "write" the life Story that we want to tell. Never give away that responsibility to someone else.

The Career Journey

A career journey starts when you have completed the interview process and you get the offer. You come home and you tell your friends and your family, "I got the job!" You landed that sales position or accounting job doing payroll, and you successfully transition into onboarding. Over the months or years, you prove to be really good at doing the job. You're a stellar individual contributor and a good team player.

An opening for a manager's job comes along, and somebody in higher management says, "You know, you're good. We want to make you a manager." You're all excited by the idea of a title and an office. In this situation, most would think that you are in control. The common belief is that you, as a manager, can now tell people what to do, that you can sit back with your feet propped on the desk, and things are going to be easy.

The reality is that you are not in control, although you can act like you are. While you may be in charge, you're not in control. When you try to control someone or something that's out of your control, that's when you lose control—*self*-control. Those unproductive behaviors such as micromanaging, making assumptions, a command-and-control approach, or a lack of delegation creep into your "management," when you are required to get work done with and through others.

In contrast to poor management, leadership means changing behaviors, moving from being an individual contributor with high technical skills to being a leader with improving-people skills. It is people skills that expand your influence. Your value to the business is now linked to your ability to get work done *with* and *through* others. In other words, your leadership skills matter the most and must be fully developed. This is The Here-to-There Journey, your Story.

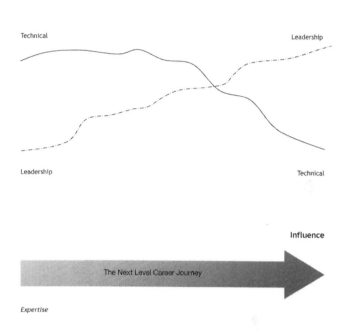

While organizations and companies need employees with expertise, the greatest need is leaders who understand people and demonstrate the ability to influence others: what could be called The People Project. Yes, leaders must know the business and do the job: oversee the work and manage systems, budgets, production, and performance. But the business of business is people. A high IQ is helpful, but emotional intelligence accounts for most of a leader's influence.

Why Leadership Development?

The Here-to-There Journey is about getting better. Three realities must be acknowledged to move forward.

THE FIRST REALITY: *What got you Here won't get you There.* The technical skills to get the job are not enough to oversee the work and lead the people.

THE SECOND REALITY: *While Here is to be celebrated, There is better.* In the Here-to-There Journey, Here is good. Congratulations! High fives! But after you've been Here for a while, the time and opportunity come to move forward or settle into a status quo or comfort zone existence. The next-level Journey is about leadership, and leadership is about expanding your personal influence to get things done with and through others. So, while Here is to be celebrated, There is the next level and is greater still.

THE THIRD REALITY: *In order to get There, something must end, or you'll be stuck Here, where you are.* Leadership development has two parts. The first part is about *engaging in a process* of change, and the second part is about *expanding your personal influence.* In other words, the why of leadership development is about expanding your personal influence, and the how and the what are about engaging in the process of change.

Leadership development is about moving from Here to There, and part of that Journey is how to expand your personal influence. It isn't about reaching a rung on the ladder, but about becoming a more effective leader.

Your Story

When it comes to the Story, you are responsible to write your Story. The question is, *are you writing the Story you want to tell?* If not, what must change?

What if we were to make an appointment three months from today? The objective would be to check in, to discover what's going on in your Story. To prepare for our one-on-one, we would need clarity regarding what needs to change for you to become a better leader.

If you want to increase your ability and capacity to lead, this book is for you. Leadership development and coaching are *unselfish attention on self for the purpose of serving better.* That's why the Here-to-There Journey is so important. I want to help you write the Story you want to tell. I've lived this. I've practiced it. I've matured with it. I'm on the journey. If this makes sense to you, and you want to engage in a process of change to expand your personal influence, it is hard. Why? Because there's a conspiracy. Before we look into that, I invite you to grab your journal and create space to reflect on "The People Project."

CREATE SPACE TO REFLECT

1. Which of the nine observations regarding people and business stand out to you?

2. Place an "X" where you see yourself on the "The Career Journey" map . Why did you place yourself there?

3. To write the Story you want to tell, what needs to change in your work as a leader? What must end? What must you stop doing to expand your personal influence?

Chapter Two

The Conspiracy

Technology can be our best friend, and technology can also be the biggest party pooper of our lives. It interrupts our own story, interrupts our ability to have a thought or a daydream, to imagine something wonderful, because we're too busy bridging the walk from the cafeteria back to the office on the cell phone.

—STEVEN SPIELBERG

We are in danger of becoming a generation of plugged in, look it uppers who are more ready to take things at face value and less willing to inquire or explore. More satisfied with proof and less open to discovery. More inclined to consume rather than create. More fearful of uncertainty than open to possibility.

—BERNADETTE JIWA

The Influence of Culture

Growing up, the message was clear: "Choose your friends wisely because you'll become like the kids you hang out with." It's easy to become so well-adjusted to the culture that we fit into it without even thinking. Sixty-years ago, a leisurely lifestyle indicated success. Now, the subtle shift has moved to busyness. Busyness has become the cultural signal of success. In their studies of this phenomenon, Silvia Bellezza of Columbia Business School, Neeru Pahari of Georgetown University and Anat Keinan of Harvard Business School have concluded, "The more we believe that one has the opportunity for success based on hard work, the more we tend to think that people who skip leisure and work all the time are of the higher standing." Addressing this change in our culture, they suggest that, "By telling others that we are busy and working all the time, we are implicitly suggesting that we are sought after, which enhances our perceived status."[1]

A Conspiracy of Silence

There appears to be an agreement in our society to keep silent about the twenty-four/seven connectivity and always-in-a-hurry lifestyle. We are committed to being so busy. It seems our culture wants us to look the other way regarding this relatively new normal of living with no margin. People have little to no time to think, to reflect, to be still and know. Author Bernadette Jiwa, a global authority on the role of story in business innovation helps us consider:

> Think about how you started your day today, and how you'll probably start it tomorrow. What was the first thing you did this morning? If you're like the average smartphone user, you reached for your phone around 7:31 a.m. Maybe you started reading email or scrolling through your Facebook feed before your feet hit the ground. Most of us check our phones within five minutes of waking and go on to check them an average of forty-six times per day.
>
> We're spending most of our waking hours reacting and responding to external inputs that we allow to steal our attention—those important, not urgent, emails and notifications that draw us in . We stopped taking time to notice and to question, to think and reflect, and just to be. And our lives and the quality of our ideas and artwork are the poorer for it.
>
> We sense opportunity all around us, and yet we don't make space to do what it takes to immerse ourselves waist high and elbow deep in the stuff that invites our curiosity and ignites our imagination—the very things that will challenge and fulfill us.[2]

Somewhat tongue-in-check author Marc Sparks book, They Can't Eat You, supports the conspiracy afoot, "There are thousands of books (mine included) written to help you do more, get more, and make more money; however, you don't see books on eliminating the noise and clutter in your life. It's human nature to amass clutter and noise."[3]

It's clear we have a problem that is increasingly difficult to hold at bay, as we're distracted by apps, notifications, multiple screens, chaos, and noise. Bestselling author Seth Godin calls technology, "Pavlov in your pocket." Further derailed by worry, fear, low self-awareness, and the acceptance of the status quo, we are pushed by our culture to pin on the "Busy!" badge, each morning. As Henry David Thoreau correctly pointed out, "It is not enough to be busy, so are the ants. The question is: What are we busy about?"[4]

Distracted Leadership

So, what gets your attention? It's easy to be confused regarding priorities, the blur of busy, and so most leaders spend their day on the *urgent*, rather than on the important, as Stephen Covey explained in The 7 Habits of Highly Effective People.

What gets your time? Is it the "job" or the "work?" By the job, I mean that untamable to-do list. The task list. The busyness that, if you're not aware, consumes not just 100 percent, but 115 percent of your time. Doug Rauch, former president of Trader Joe's, illustrates the danger zone, if you don't create space to think: "In my zeal to control everything, I kept micromanaging. The effect was stifling." The **job** is all that stuff that consumes your day and has you wondering what you accomplished, at the end of the day.[5]

In contrast to the job, your **work** as a leader is to create value. Adding value requires creating space to think, to keep the vision alive, to keep the culture on track, and to keep the mission and value of the organization alive in employees' heads and hearts.

The Reality

What happens when you ask someone, "How are you?" I find the typical response is not even a superficial, "I'm doing fine," but more often, I hear,

"I'm so busy." The pace of life leaves us with less margin each passing day. And when the *pace of life* is out of control, that leads to out-of-control lives, families, and work places. When the pace of life is out of control, it limits our ability to be creative, to be innovative, to connect and care for one another as people. However, there is a pace that liberates instead of limits. This is counterintuitive. In leadership development terms, we have to *slow down to accelerate*. Why? Because it takes time to think. It takes time to reflect on truth (feedback, experience, success, and failure) found in the Story. Create space at the beginning of your day, or you will lose your day to the tyranny of the urgent.

You must create space to see the people in your life. It's so easy to see employees—people—as cogs in the machine. (Business eats people.) How well do you celebrate and appreciate the people on your team? Leaders who create space are more likely to experience breakthrough performance.

Basic Resistance to Change

In an interesting article, "Ten Reasons People Resist Change," Rosabeth Moss Kanter suggests the most common reasons people resist change:[6]

1. LOSS OF CONTROL. Change seems to interfere with one's sense of self-determination. So, we fear loss of control.

2. EXCESS UNCERTAINTY. It's easier to stay in the comfort zone; even if we are miserable, it's easier. Uncertainty about change makes it harder to embrace—and easier to resist.

3. LOSS OF COMFORT. How different will it really be? I've got my habits, my routines. This is the way we've always done it. What's really going to happen?

4. LOSS OF FACE. What we know is what we've done. It's the past and we're getting ready to depart from the past. What if I can't keep up? What if I can't get it?

5. CONCERNS ABOUT COMPETENCE. Can I make this change? Can I understand this new way of doing business? Can I comprehend this new software? Am I competent?

6. MORE WORK. It almost goes without saying that when we make changes, we still must do what we were doing, while onboarding the new methods. Whether it's software or process or new people, more work goes with the territory. It's easier to leave it all alone.

7. RIPPLE EFFECTS. Unintended consequences of a decision and far-reaching ripples of change can impact the company in ways we didn't even think about.

8. PAST RESENTMENTS. Political games and buried resentments come back to haunt us. Now, it's a chance to "stick it to you, because I remember what you did to me."

9. SOMETIMES, THERE IS RESISTANCE TO CHANGE BECAUSE THE THREAT IS REAL. Change can and will upset the way we do things.

The Pain

What happens if you don't create space? Consider what Doug, an executive in the automotive industry says, "Leaders are just caught up in the rush, rush, rush, and they're looking for an outlet to be able to admit, 'I can't get all this done. How am I going to get it all done?' Then, when you create space, you realize you might be doing the wrong things, and that's why you can't get the right things done." So, what are the consequences if we don't create space? You might recognize some of these.

1. We become less aware of what's going on in our Story. Within the Story is the truth, the reality, and facts that you have to consider to be able to lead change, or to lead at all.

2. We fail to appreciate and see the people in the Story, due to the pace and the busyness of life. It's already hard to see people and to celebrate and appreciate them.

3. We're more inclined to do the unthinkable—we won't see the whole picture until it is too late.

4. We settle for unproductive behavior, because it takes time and effort to change the behavior.

5. We fail to do the right thing for the right reasons.

6. When we don't create space, we can expect strained relationships, unnecessary stress, conflict, and unfulfilled expectations. The result is frustration.

What Can Hinder Your Future Success?

Life happens in the Here-to-There Journey. Life disrupts our plans. Disruption of plans calls for change. Do we resist the call to change and move forward differently? Or do we use special tactics to avoid the truth that we must change? All of us will recognize some of these tactics:

1. BLAME: Placing responsibility on someone else

2. DENIAL: Refusing to acknowledge what's going on

3. RATIONALIZATION: Making excuses, avoiding responsibility

4. MINIMIZATION: Underestimating intentionally, "It's no big deal."

5. AVOIDANCE: Withdrawing from the situation or avoiding the person

Having acknowledged the battle for our attention, consider the following questions before we take a trip to the moon and learn how to deal with the distractions that can steal our best work.

CREATE SPACE TO REFLECT

1. What's the "new normal" in your life that limits you?

2. Where do you see, "I'm so busy" taking its toll on your life?

3. What are the top three distractions that interrupt your life and work?

4. Of the five common responses to accepting responsibility, which can drive your resistance to change?

5. Where are you hearing the call to change in your Story?

6. Which of the ten reasons for resisting change do you identify with?

Chapter Three
Take Me to The Moon

Life is not a problem to be solved, but a reality to be experienced.
—Soren Kierkegaard

Since we cannot change reality, let us change the eyes which see reality.
—Nikos Kazantzakis

Twelve people have walked on the moon. Do you know what happens to someone who travels into outer space? James Irwin, the eighth man to walk on the moon on the Apollo XV mission, described the earth as fragile and delicate. "As we got further and further away, it diminished in size. Finally, it shrank to the size of a marble. The most beautiful you can imagine. To see this has to *change* a man." Canada's first female astronaut Roberta Bondar reported, "To fly in space is to *see the reality* of earth alone. The experience *changed* my life and my attitude toward life itself." The Journey to a new perspective changes the traveler.

For most of us, it's very difficult, if not impossible, to comprehend the size of the universe. The Apollo XI astronauts gained perspective when they stood on the moon and looked down and could block out the entire earth with their thumb. This moment led Neil Armstrong to describe feeling "very, very small." The "Overview Effect" is a mental clarity or euphoria that astronauts feel when looking at earth from orbit. The Overview Institute's website describes the Overview Effect as "the experience of seeing firsthand the reality of the Earth in space, which is immediately understood to be a tiny, fragile ball of life, hanging in the void, shielded and nourished by a paper-thin atmosphere."[7]

The Overview Effect, a term first coined and described by author Frank White, in 1987, is an experience that *transforms* an astronaut's *perspective* of the planet and mankind's place upon it. "Common features of the experience are a feeling of awe for the planet, a profound understanding of the interconnection of all life, and a renewed sense of responsibility for taking care of the environment. Having traveled into space, they return home different."[8] Better.

If Earth-gazing can change a person's life, imagine what could happen when you create space for life-gazing. Creating space to think, to listen, to reflect on the Story you are writing—one year, one month, one day, at a time.

David Yaden, a research scientist at the University of Pennsylvania, asks how we can get a taste of the Overview Effect without leaving the confines of gravity. "We don't need to go to space to benefit from intense experiences of awe," Yaden says. "We can experience a little bit of the Overview Effect on mountain tops or by viewing a beautiful sunset. There are a lot of opportunities for these experiences that are all around us."[9] So put down the smartphone. Go outside and take in the view. Glance up at the stars and ponder your existence on our own pale blue dot, and let the awe wash over you.

Creating space is a bit like taking a trip to the moon. As you know, the pace of life is chaotic, busy, noisy, with limited margin. There's a whole lot of doing; there's a lot going on. That's life on the blue marble. When you create space, you intentionally interrupt the doing to think. When you "take a trip to the moon," it helps you gain perspective, increase self-awareness, stand in awe of the opportunity to lead, and yes, notice what you had taken for granted or missed seeing. More specifically, to create space involves the disciplined use of time, location, and resources to reflect on the truth you find in your Story.

Hidden in Plain Sight

The clue to staying alive to the wonder of life and your Story is found in the word space. When you look at the word *space*, you'll also find the word pace. To create space, you must take charge of the pace of life, or it will control you.

P.A.C.E. Yourself

Greek writer and nominee for the Nobel Prize in Literature Nikos Kazantzakis reminds us, "Since we cannot change reality, let us change the eyes which see reality, says one of my favorite Byzantine mystics. I did this when a child; I do it now as well in the most creative moments of my life." To see differently requires us to pace ourselves. What does it mean to "pace yourself"?[10] The answer is found tucked away in space: P.A.C.E.

- PAUSE AND BREATHE: When human beings feel a threat or fear, we have a biological response that puts us into high alert and puts us into fight-or-flight mode. So, when feeling threatened, the first thing to do is pause and breathe.

- ASK QUESTIONS: When we ask questions, we're creating space to think within the moment. For example, asking questions of ourselves like the following: "Why am I afraid right now?" "Why do I feel threatened?" "What's really going on?" "What do I believe?" Ask questions about the Story. Of course, you could ask questions of the other person to gain understanding.

- CHALLENGE BELIEFS: What are you accepting as true? How do you know it's true? What's the truth in the Story?

- EDIT THE STORY: There are three questions you can ask when trying to edit the Story. (1) What happened? (2) What did I want to happen? (3) How would I need to show up for that to happen?

When we create space to think about the Story and look for truth in the Story, we observe from a historical perspective by asking, "What happened?" It takes time to think about it. However, the practice can set you up for future success by reflecting on how you want to show up next time. Consider what questions you would ask, next time. Explore whether it would have been better to postpone the conversation and schedule a meeting at another time. To edit the Story involves reviewing what happened, so you can perform better next time.

As a leader who creates space, you will be more inclined to focus on what matters. You will have a better understanding of what's going on around you, which allows you to be more responsive and less reactive. You will connect the dots between unproductive behavior and how it limits your leadership. You will choose the ethical path and do the right thing for the right reason; you've created space to think, so you're less likely to do the unthinkable.

It's possible to develop the ability to pace yourself and then reap the rewards. You will notice opportunities to work on unproductive behavior. You'll take responsibility to write the Story you want to tell.

When you P.A.C.E. yourself and create space to think, your influence will expand, allowing you to achieve breakthrough performance in life and work.

The Three C's of Next-Level Leaders

Remember, leaders create space to think, first for themselves, then for others. Leaders create space in a variety of ways to sustain their effectiveness by intentionally interrupting their "doing." Then they are able to listen, think, and reflect. The pace and challenges of business and life require this discipline. So, what is it that the next-level leaders do? There are three practical ways they expand their influence with other people.

First, they **connect** with others. The goal of connecting is to *discover the Story* by being mindful and asking questions. The simple, yet powerful question is "What got us here?"

Second, they **create**. Here, the goal is to *explore the potential*. And the question to ask is "What does 'There' look like in our Journey from Here to There?" Engage others with hope that the Story holds excitement, growth, and opportunity.

Third, they **coach**. This goal is to have compassion and *care for the person*. The question is "How do we get There?" Specifically, how can I help you get to your next level, your *There*?

In their book, *Resonant Leadership*, Richard Boyatzis and Annie McKee write about how to create and sustain resonance in difficult times. The question is *how do you take care of yourself as a leader and cultivate effective relationships?* Their research suggests three key ideas.

1. MINDFUL: The authors describe effective leaders saying, "They seek to live in full consciousness of self, others, nature, and society."

2. HOPEFUL: "They inspire through clarity of vision, optimism, and a profound belief in their people's ability to turn dreams into reality."

3. COMPASSIONATE: Leaders "face sacrifice, difficulties, and challenges, as well as opportunities, with empathy and compassion for the people they lead and serve."[11]

The Journey from being a skilled individual contributor to being a manager with increased responsibilities is about much more than just a title or a position or power. It is about how you expand and use your influence with people. How do you get things done with and through others? How do you get better and build something great?

The Possibilities

Leadership development has two parts. There is the WHY of leadership development, which is to *expand your personal influence*. And there is the HOW of leadership development, which is to *engage in a process of change*. Leaders create space to think and clarity to act. When they do, they can create the opportunity to get better.

To do this creative work of leadership requires your transformation as a leader and your ability to transform disruption into clarity for life and work. For example, Jay is a frontline manager on your team. You've received feedback from his team that he operates as a micromanager. He delegates, but doesn't let go. The "truth in the Story" is it's Jay's way or the highway. Top talent are frustrated. You deliver the feedback to Jay, who, by the way, is blind to his control freak tendencies. Jay's career will be limited unless he changes this stifling behavior. Jay's belief about this "disruption" will affect his future. Will he react or respond to the feedback? Will this be something that has happened to *him* or *for him*? If he is able to P.A.C.E. himself, he will create space to think. Presenting him with the facts of the Story gives him the opportunity to engage in a change to his behavior and expand his influence. His future success depends on what he believes about the feedback.

A trip to the moon allows you to get a new point of view, to gain perspective, to take the Here-to-There Journey. As Dr. Seuss wrote, in his children's book — Oh, the Places You'll Go! "You're off to great places, today's your day. Your mountain is waiting, so get on your way." Next , we'll look into the adventure ahead on your journey and how to embrace change. But first, grab your journal and let's create space to reflect right now.[12]

CREATE SPACE TO THINK

1. The Overview Effect speaks to the change in perspective astronauts experience. How might you benefit from a trip to the moon?

2. When do you stand in awe?

3. Here are a few of the benefits that are available when you create space. Which benefit do you want to have more of?

   - Time to reflect and pursue truth in the Story

   - An increased ability and willingness to embrace feedback, experience, success, and failure as truth in the Story

   - Development of a long view of personal growth and a process that supports it

- The ability to see the people
- Increased gratitude, appreciation, and celebration of others
- A sharper focus on what really matters

Chapter Four
The Here-to-There Journey

What we call the process, God calls the objective.
—OSWALD CHAMBERS

*Everyone thinks of changing the world but no one
thinks of changing himself.*
—LEO TOLSTOY

*Sustainable transformations follow a predictable pattern
of build-up and breakthrough.*
—JIM COLLINS

"I want to stand on top of the world," he told his family and friends. For the son of a beekeeper, that would be an ambitious aspiration. His climbing experience began as a high school student. Although he followed in his father's footsteps as a beekeeper, he wanted more adventure in his Story. Following a tour of duty during World War II, he returned home determined to achieve his goal, which could mean nothing less than to summit the most famous mountain in the world, Mount Everest.

The thirty-four-year-old New Zealand beekeeper, along with Sherpa Tenzing Norgay, set out to reach the top on May 29, 1953. As a Sherpa, Tenzing served as a highly skilled and experienced climber and mountain guide in the Everest area. Tenzing's role was important to the beekeeper's success. Together, they set out to reach the South Summit. Edmund Hillary and Tenzing Norgay completed the 29,035 feet climb, reaching the summit of Mount Everest that morning. The "men shook hands; Tenzing then embraced Hillary in a hug. Hillary took photos. Tenzing, a Buddhist, made an offering of food for the mountain; Hillary left a crucifix Hunt had given him. The two men ate some sweets and then headed down. They had spent about fifteen minutes on the top of the world."

The incredible journey to conquer Mount Everest was achieved. Upon his return to London that July, he was knighted, Sir Edmund Hillary, as one of the men responsible for the successful journey and achievement.[13]

The Connection

Each Here-to-There Journey is a part of your Story. In chapter two, I introduced the five realities of the Story.

- *Everyone* has a Story.
- Every day you *add* to the Story.
- Today, you will *influence* someone's Story.
- There's always *more to* the Story, and
- You are responsible to *write your* Story.

One reason paying attention to the Story is so important is because we find truth in the Story. What do I mean by truth? In this context, I do not mean the Truth as revealed in Scripture, although very beneficial. For the purpose of personal growth and development, truth is the facts and reality. What *really* happened? Truth includes feedback, experience, success, and failure. To move forward successfully, we must have truth. To accept something as true when it is not true is deception or denial, and leaves us stuck Here.

Another benefit of paying attention to the Story is how it connects us as people. When you take a stroll through your life, notice all the people who have influenced you. The Story connects us as family, employees, team members, or citizens. Remember, you are continually writing a Story, and the big question is, "Are you writing the Story you want to tell?"

The third benefit of the Story is how it instructs us when we listen. This is one reason why leaders create space, to connect with people and with truth, so they can make the Journey and enjoy the adventure of life.

The Three Zones

On the Here-to-There Journey, you'll notice there are three zones. The first zone is the comfort zone. You know the territory. The work is not challenging, the role is familiar, comfortable, low risk. What happens when we stay in the comfort zone? We settle for a nonthreatening life, for status quo behavior, for status quo performance.

Alasdair White writes in his research paper, *From Comfort Zone to Performance Management*, "A comfort zone is a behavioral state within which a person operates in an anxiety neutral condition using a limited set of behaviors to deliver a steady level of performance, usually without a sense of risk."[14] It's the difference between the workout with my trainer at the gym and when I'm there on my own. Again, comfortable.

Once we look to the future and see the potential and the possibilities, there are two things that move us out of our comfort zone, *pain* and *promise*. How interesting that we call someplace a comfort zone, when in reality, it may be painful. Part of the reason we can stay in a painful situation is because people have a high pain tolerance. Soon, we begin to accept the unhealthy habit, unproductive behavior, the chaos as the new norm, when the opportunity for growth, the potential to get better, waits for us to respond. To leave a comfort zone means we must overcome fear. You see, fear stands at the gate holding back all the "citizens of Stuckville." What calls us to break out of a comfort zone is the idea of promise. Promise reminds us we can get better, do better, be transformed. Our team can perform better. We'll come back to that.

The second zone is the **safety zone**. This is when you feel the risk, but go for it. To illustrate this, go to any corner in a city and what do you find? As a pedestrian, you can walk in the street and stare down a car or be run over by it. However, a pedestrian crosswalk is designed to be a

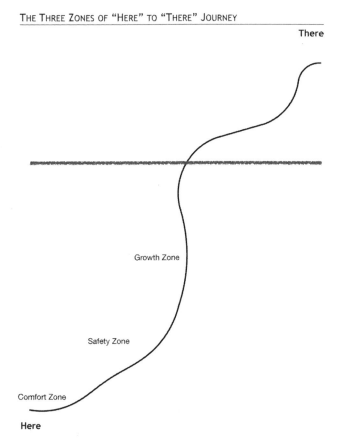

THE THREE ZONES OF "HERE" TO "THERE" JOURNEY

There

Growth Zone

Safety Zone

Comfort Zone

Here

safety zone. There is still a risk, but it is a safer place for pedestrians to move from one side of the street to the other—to go from one place to another, Here to There.

Having made it to the safety zone, you're a small step from entrance into the **growth zone**. The growth zone is where you exercise your ability and willingness to learn and change. One of the great attributes of being human is that you don't have to live in Stuckville (the comfort zone). You can grow. You can develop. You can change the way you think. You can develop new skills and new habits that support your success. You can be transformed and become someone different, someone better than you were a week ago, or six months ago, or a year ago. It's the power of being human.

Three Questions to Explore

To explore your Here-to-There Journey use these three simple questions about your adventure: First, What got me Here? Then, What does There look like? And the last question to explore is How will I get There? Your response will reveal where you need to engage change and expose your willingness to move forward.

Three Realities of the Journey

As you acknowledge the Here-to-There Journey, part of the resistance can come from your previous success. "Why do I need to change? Do you know who I am? Have you any idea how I got this position? What you want me to stop doing is what got me this corner office." It's easy to think, "What I've been doing got me here, so why would I want to change?"

Consider the following realities of the Here-to-There Journey.

First, *what got you Here will not get you There.* Obviously, what you've done has allowed you to achieve success, to get where you are today, to perform well. But what got you Here will not—with new responsibilities, a new role, a new team—get you There, or you'd be There now!

A second reality to face is *while Here is to be celebrated, There is better.* This requires an element of faith and open mindedness. Again, your ability and willingness to learn and change will be tested. What if there's a more effective way to communicate? How willing are your to explore another approach?

The last reality makes it clear that *in order to get There, something must end or you'll be stuck Here.* If we go back to our illustration of micromanagement, you may have been a micromanager for ten years and have been promoted multiple times. However, as you move up in the organization, talented people will not submit to being micromanaged. They want to be led and given authority to get things done. They want to be empowered. Emerging leaders and high-potentials want to be given the objectives and then the freedom to go and do whatever it takes to meet them. To fail, even.

As we think about the Here-to-There Journey, we're not talking about the ladder, but the leader and how to develop the "soft skills" to become a more successful leader.

The Four Phases of Change

As you hear the call to change and you're willing to engage in a process of change to expand your personal influence, there are four phases of change that can help you map change as a process. These steps are applicable whether for you, as an individual leader, or for the team you lead or the organization you run.

The first phase is **desire,** a strong feeling of wanting something. When it comes to desire, have you ever wanted something for somebody else more than he or she wanted it? How did that work out? Often when we desire change for someone, even for their benefit, it doesn't work because the desire has to come from within. Remember, often it requires both pain and promise to embrace change.

Discipline, the second phase required for change, is a systematic method for getting something done. When we train ourselves to do something by developing new habits, that's discipline. For example, returning to our micromanager who was recently promoted, her desire to delegate and let go of her old ways as a micromanager are critical to her success. The corresponding discipline is practice and persistence in delegating. Delegation of a task requires 80 percent clearly set objectives and 20 percent leeway. The ability to let go of that 20 percent (how she would do it) and delegate the project to an individual or team is key to the discipline that will permit our manager to succeed.

The third phase of change is **determination**, a sense of firmness or level of commitment. Determination is being intentional about moving forward. It is so easy to fall back into old habits! So, for our micromanager, when the pressure begins, the stress builds, and when the deadline is looming, it's easy for our micromanager to revert to her old habit, that is, until the new habit of delegation and the mindset of delegating are second nature to her. This is the time when courage is required to experience a breakthrough. It's so easy to slip back into old habits, thought patterns or beliefs. When the resistance comes (and it will) when it's hard to finish, you've got to show up with mental and morale strength to preserver and withstand fear. Determination and courage until the breakthrough happens.

Delight is the last of the four phases of change. Desire. Discipline. Determination. Delight, the joy you experience when something pleases you. We love it, or at least we like it. It's not only the satisfaction of a victory, but that you are more enjoyable to be around. It is a delight when a micromanager learns to delegate. The truth in the Story is how her influence with the team expands with appreciation for her new leadership skill.

To help you remember this, I'd like for you to think of a Snickers candy bar. Got it? Imagine, as you lift your eyes from reading this page, you see a Snickers bar that has magically appeared on your desk. What begins to happen as you look at the Snickers? If you like Snickers like I like Snickers, you *desire* that Snickers, but nothing happens if you just sit there and look at it. The desire calls for some action. You're *disciplined*. So, being a highly disciplined person, you reach to pick up the Snickers. With great *determination*, you wrestle with that adult-proof wrapper and release the delicious smell of chocolate. Your mouth begins to water. Then, with great discipline and determination, you sink your teeth into that fresh milk chocolate and caramel and peanuts and nougat. Surely, you're in a state of great *delight*. Would you like coffee with that?

Now to recap, the *four phases of change* are desire, discipline, determination, and delight. As you go through the checkout at the store, remember the Snickers message. Let it help you remember the four phases of change required to take your Here-to-There Journey.

What's Stopping You?

On this Journey from Here to There, even when you make it to the growth zone, there will be resistance. There will be pushback, either internally or externally driven. Resistance is an opposing force. It could be refusal to accept something new or different, or to refuse to hear the call for change. Resistance is any effort or force trying to stop you in your tracks. You know about this resistance.

In terms of leadership development and unproductive behavior, there is a long list of things that can hold us back from expanding our influence. Leadership development is engaging in a process of change, to expand our personal influence. The breakthrough comes as we identify and change our unproductive behaviors that limit our connection with others.

Some things that come to mind when thinking about unproductive behavior include the following: ineffective communication, micromanagement, lack of integrity, perfectionism, poor listening skills, intimidation, low trust, manipulation, defensiveness, failure to delegate, unrealistic expectations, and a lack of praise and appreciation for others. It's easy to become comfortable with such behaviors. Micromanagement is not a helpful tool when you're trying to lead highly talented people, but it's what got you where you are, so you could be comfortable with it, or even unaware of it. When your next-level opportunity comes (perhaps a promotion from individual contributor to team leader), it will call for some level of change.

The Thrill of Victory

In the Here-to-There Journey, we've discussed the progression of moving from a comfort zone to a safety zone to a growth zone. Next, we covered moving from desire to discipline, from discipline to determination, from determination to delight. When we achieve a breakthrough we experience the delight of victory.

A breakthrough is about overcoming an obstacle or something that holds us back. It's about removing barriers to progress. Let's revisit our friend the micromanager. Whether she realizes it or not, micromanaging limits her potential, her influence with others, and her ultimate success. The breakthrough is about getting results by eliminating this unproductive behavior.

In the Here-to-There Journey, two conditions support you as you break out of the comfort zone: *pain* and *promise*. The adventure is not experienced staying at base camp sitting around the fire. If you are growth oriented, want to be transformed in the way that you show up in life, personally and professionally, then you must embrace that there is some area of change required to expand your personal influence, to achieve greater results and success, and improve your performance as a leader. After all, you want to stand on top of the world!

Next we explore the role disruption plays in writing the Story we want to tell. But first, dig a little deeper in your journey with these questions.

CREATE SPACE TO THINK

1. Which zone are you in now—your comfort zone, safety zone, or growth zone? What will it take for you to move forward?

2. What's your "red line" behavior that may hold you back?

3. There are four phases of change—desire, discipline, determination, and delight. Where are you?

4. What does There look like in your development and work as a leader? Where do you want to become a better leader?

Chapter Five

The Gift of Disruption

When you disrupt yourself, you are looking for growth, so if you want to muscle up a curve, you have to push and pull against objects and barriers that would constrain and constrict you. That is how you get stronger.

— WHITNEY JOHNSON

I love water features—the gurgling sounds and dance moves of the water. The music of the waterfall and the graceful, silent movement of my Japanese koi. We built our first backyard pond in 1984. I was an amateur. We filled it with a unique variety of water life. The inhabitants came from a local bait shop; you know, minnows, perch, waterdogs, a catfish, even a small gar made for a delightful experience.

With each revision, design and quality improved. In 2008, we purchased our current home, which provided the setup for the ultimate koi pond. My vision included a fourteen-foot winding stream delivering biologically filtered water, joyfully splashing down a four-foot waterfall. The 3200 gallons of clear water recycled every hour, providing the residents a perfect home and entertainment for all to enjoy.

It started as a vision penciled out on a sheet of notebook paper. The story of how we got tons of native rock donated and delivered and how the big rocks were stacked in place was a once-in-a-lifetime experience. Each week, we made progress. It was really looking good.

One Saturday, I was looking forward to moving the project along, when it rained. Ugh. To say I was disappointed would be an understatement. While eating lunch and looking out the window at the construction site, I noticed something was missing. The retaining wall would be about five feet tall and currently, would not allow access to the stream bed! The rain had disrupted the project and created space to think, to discover, to explore, to improve, to *change* the plan. Because the rain disrupted the work, we built steps into the retaining wall, giving it character and providing access. The disruption had allowed me to create something better. Let it rain!

Disruption

Disruption is what happens on your way to your goals, on your way from Here to There. Like Edmond Hillary's adventure, Mount Everest expeditions are disrupted by storms, changes in the weather, high winds, falling temperatures, avalanches, and physical limitations brought on by severe exhaustion or dehydration or altitude sickness. While building our koi pond, disruption came when it rained, and I wanted to be busy, working on the project. You want to work, to make progress, to be productive! You're busy—who has time to think? Disruption is an interruption that disturbs the plan; it shows up as resistance or opposition. Disruption is the rain in your Story, on your way to build something better or become a better version of yourself. Whether it's your life, your work as a leader, or your business, disruption is the obstacle you will face when you choose to leave your comfort zone to step into the safety zone and then the growth zone.

Perhaps the limitation of underperformance is what disrupts your Journey. Perhaps it's what is going on in your profession or your sector of business or your industry. The disruption could be a decision that must be made, if you're going to move forward. The mission of a disruption is to get our attention and call us to change.

Something Happens

How do you experience disruption? From my observation, most people see it as a negative. The disruption is something that happens "to me." If we interpret disruption this way, as something that happened "to me," it's much more likely you'll *react* and increase the stress level. When the disruption has happened "to you," it's easy to become defensive. This invites conflict between people, which limits progress. In the Here-to-There Journey, you'll be a Stuckville resident, unless you interrupt doing to think, because it's easy to keep doing the same thing and expecting something different. When disruption happens, it's easy to make a U-turn and head back to your comfort zone.

When disruption comes it's a call to change. What could hinder your progress from moving forward? Your response. When the call to change comes, how do you respond? When the truth in the Story indicates it's your behavior that limits your influence, how do you respond?

Transformation

In the Here-to-There Journey, we start out in the comfort zone or "Stuckville." To break out of your comfort zone requires two things: one is the truth; the other is time.

THE THREE CREATIONS OF LEADERSHIP FOR BREAKTHROUGH PERFORMANCE

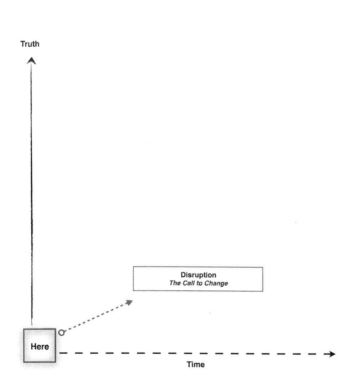

Time helps us structure life. We measure time in minutes and hours. As an intentional portion of time allotted for a specific purpose. To break out of a comfort zone, we must create space to think, schedule time to think about where we are and where we want to be—and yes, what must end to move forward.

Regarding truth, we're talking about the facts in the Story, the reality. Not just your reality, but the true reality. Truth is obtained through feedback, observation, experience, success, and failure. When we invest time in the *pursuit* of truth, it moves us closer and closer to our breakthrough and enables us to make the Here-to-There Journey. If you plot the amount of time given to think and the desire for truth, you'll see how likely you are to experience a breakthrough as a leader or as a team or an organization.

Disruption is a reality for everyone who takes the Here-to-There Journey. To move toward a breakthrough, you must disrupt the disruption, that is, "intentionally interrupt doing, to think." It's too easy to keep beating your head against the wall and to resist change, to repeat the same behavior, while expecting a different result. The intentional interruption of doing to create space to think will help us see things we're missing, like adding the stairs to my landscape project. Disruption is about an opportunity. Disruption happens "for me," instead of "to me." Instead of fighting it, I'm free to embrace it as something that offers possibilities, innovation, a creative opportunity, or a chance to get better.

When we view disruption as something that happens *for me*, we're free to *respond*, to *engage* the Story, to learn and change, to own our responsibility in the disruption, to think about solutions, and to look for the possibilities. The questions we ask when we're in that frame of mind move from "Why me?" to "What am I missing? How could this be better? How could I get better? What do I need to change? How will I show up differently?" When we create space for an active disruption, we intentionally interrupt our doing to think.

What can be perceived as a setback can become the moment that you move forward. When you step out of the insanity loop, and are willing to leave your comfort zone and step into the safety zone and then your growth zone, the setback becomes the stimulus to breakout of Stuckville to find a better place—yes, to move from Here to There. As a leader, this moves you from a shrinking influence to an expanding personal influence because you're willing to engage in change. This all adds to your future success or produces your future success following a breakthrough.

The Power of Thinking

Follow social media posts and tweets and news headlines, and it's clear that "people don't think." Everyday, we do the unthinkable, for a lack of thought. And yet it is true thinking affects our performance and lives. As best selling author and leadership expert John Maxwell writes in his book, Thinking for a Change, "Your thinking, more than anything else, shapes the way you live. It's really true that if you change your thinking, you can change your life." British author James Allen reminds us in his book, Above Life's Turmoil, "You are today where your thoughts have brought you. You will be tomorrow where your thoughts take you." Clearly, it is important for you to create space to think.

In the pursuit of a life well lived, Maxwell identifies the link between six actions that lead to future success in life. It's about disruption's call to change. Where do you need and desire improvement in your life or business? Precision in identifying what you want to change is required.

Then, the first action is to change what you **think** about the disruption, feedback, experience, success, or failure. *What do you think about the situation, person, or challenge?*

Changing your thinking allows you to change what you **believe**, the second action. *What are you accepting as true? How do you know it's true? Is it possible?*

Changing your belief allows the third action, which is to change your **expectations**. Based on what you are thinking and accepting as true, what do you expect to happen?

Changing your expectations affects your **attitude**, the fourth action. *What do you feel? What's your personal view about this situation or person or assignment? What is your attitude toward the necessary change?*

Changing your attitude supports changes in your **behavior**. *How are you showing up? How do the people that you work with or live with experience you? What's your behavior? Does it to lead toward success, or does it minimize your opportunity because the behavior becomes your performance?*

Changing your behavior leads to a change in your **performance**, the sixth and last action. Change what you think, what you believe, what you expect, your attitude, and your behavior and watch your performance improve. Your performance becomes your life— the Story you are writing.[15]

To write the Story you want to tell, pay attention, create space to think. David Schwartz, author of *The Magic of Thinking Big*, helps us make the connection between success and our thinking. "Where success is concerned, people are not measured in inches, or pounds, or college degrees, or family background; they are measured by the size of their thinking."

It's What You Believe

Here is a very simple, but powerful, equation: **ev + b = em.**

Ev represents an **event**—something that happened; it could represent a person or a truth. The *b* stands for **belief**—what I think about and accept as true about, or my expectations regarding, the event. And *em* represents **emotion**—it will be fear based or faith based, negative or positive, frustration or anticipation. What we have in this equation is: **Event + Belief = Emotion.**

When you look at that equation, you find only one variable you can control, and that's what you **believe**. The event is out of your control, it's history. Whatever the event was, plus what you believe or accept as true, produces an emotion. That emotion will be either positive or negative.

What you think and believe changes the outcome. For example, "I believe Joe is a jerk." The result or emotion? "I'm so frustrated with him." Or you believe, "This disruption happened 'to me' or 'for me,' and therefore, I have hope that I will gain insight as I create space to think; I'm excited to see what's going to happen next and how to get better." What if Joe turns out to be someone I can influence? How does my behavior contribute to our conflict?

Procrastination

There are two types of procrastination. Destructive procrastination involves being easily distracted and delayed. It's when we avoid the stress of taking action, avoiding a decision because of fear. As best selling author Seth Godin says, "Fear is a dream killer. It puts people into suspended animation, holding their breath, paralyzed, and unable to move forward." Destructive procrastination causes people to maintain residence in Stuckville, to stay in the comfort zone, where status quo thinking and behavior, reinforced by fear, blocks the exit. "I'll start moving soon, just not today."

There is also a productive procrastination, which happens when you intentionally interrupt doing, to think. When an obstacle, indecision, or underperformance freezes you in your tracks on your Here-to-There Journey, remember to embrace disruption as a call to change. Only when you create space to think, will you be free to find solutions, make changes, and build something better.

In part two, we'll identify the three creations of leadership that can transform disruption into breakthrough performance. Here are some questions to use as you create space to think about disruption as a gift.

CREATE SPACE TO THINK

1. When has disruption been a gift in your Story? What happened? What changed? How did you benefit from the disruption?

2. What's your first response to disruption? Is it something has happened to *me* or *for me*?

3. Think of a recent story when you were frustrated. Why did you feel frustrated? What did you believe about the person or situation? Explore the story; what happens if you change what you believe?

Part Two:

The Three Creations of Leadership

Chapter Six

The Discipline to Create Space

Right discipline consists not in external compulsion, but in the habits of mind which lead spontaneously to desirable, rather than undesirable, activities.
—BERTRAND RUSSELL

Step outside and look around. Walk through a forest or sit in a beautiful garden. Everywhere you look, there are plants. Now, consider their journey. On appearance, a seed does not encourage hope for the future, and yet a seed contains enough life to sprout when given water. With the promise of life, the process is initiated, as tiny roots appear.

The seed's potential for growth is placed in what appears to be a disadvantageous situation. The seed could believe the soil is opposing its future success, being buried is part of the opposition's plan to defeat it, but we know it is part of life's plan. The buried seed's outer shell is softened, allowing the seed to take in nutrients until it breaks through the earth, and a small plant emerges. With light, food, and water, the first stages of its development begin.

The transformation happens before our very eyes. What was once dormant is awakened to develop, grow, and be productive, to perform its role in Creation.

Producing Breakthrough Performance

The Here-to-There Journey engages us in a process of change designed to expand our personal influence. Along the Journey, there are obstacles. In the previous chapter, we named one of these obstacles as disruption, which can be experienced as resistance, a challenge, unproductive behavior, or underperformance. Whatever it's called, there is no question that it's part of the Story. Disruption is a *call to change*, an invitation to get better. Your full contribution in life depends on development. To experience breakthrough performance, you must embrace disruption and see the promise of There. Disruption can become an expression of your life, marked by potential and possibility. The question is will you exercise your ability and willingness to learn and change?

I know you've made this Journey before, or you would not be holding this book in your hands. The goal of *Leaders Create Space* is to provide a natural process and map, so you can experience intentional breakthroughs as a leader and with your team. The Journey requires knowing where you are, where you want to go, and how you'll get there. To produce breakthrough performance, you must meet disruption with three creative acts. The first one is to create space to think, the second, to create clarity to act, and the third, to create opportunity to get better.

Creating the Space

So, what does it take to experience a breakthrough in your performance? The first act is to create space: *the disciplined use of time, place, and resources.* It means to listen for truth in the Story, and to reflect on what's happening.

Time. Time is how we prioritize what matters most, how we schedule an appointment to listen for truth in the Story. To think.

Place. Not only when, but where will you shut the door on busyness and all the distractions and the noise in order to listen and become a pursuer of truth?

Resources. They're in the Story. They're also books, a coach, a mate or teammate, that friend. Everything that goes on in your life that can help you gain wisdom, insight, and understanding is a resource.

Truth in the Story. The facts are reality. Yes, I know people who have their own realities, but we're looking for what really happened in the

THE THREE CREATIONS OF LEADERSHIP FOR BREAKTHROUGH PERFORMANCE

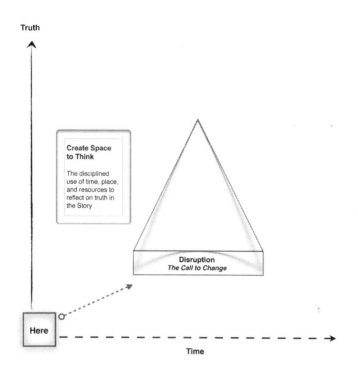

Story. We also call it feedback, experience, success, and especially failure. When preacher, entrepreneur, and author T.D. Jakes talks about his Story, he says he found blessing in brokenness and success amid failure. As he eloquently described it, "We mature to realize that we grow more in our suffering than we do in our success. Our success is just a distraction from the class of suffering, where we are developed as human beings. And I hate it as much as anybody in the world, but everything I've ever learned that mattered, I learned it from failure and falling and suffering. I celebrated success, but I learned it in suffering."[16]

So how do you approach disruption? Remember, the goal is to embrace disruption, to *respond* positively. It is a call to change the unproductive behavior, underperformance, indecision, and unsolved problems that hold you back from going from Here to There. This Journey is yours, your team's, or your entire organization's. Remember T-n-T (time-n-truth) is required to break out of Stuckville, that is, time—the intentional interruption of doing to think — and truth — feedback, experience, success, and failure. Some think "leadership" and "vulnerability" don't belong in the same sentence. Brené Brown, in her book, *Daring Greatly* clarifies reality, "Vulnerability sounds like truth and feels like courage. Truth and courage aren't always comfortable, but they're never weakness."

So what do you spend your time doing? When do you listen and reflect on truth in the Story? When do you close the gap between "my truth" and what really happened? The focus is on the Story. As we look at our diagram, you'll see the circle inside the triangle. The Story informs us along the next-level Journey of producing breakthrough performance.

It takes time to create space to think and humility to listen for truth in the Story. Truth directs us along the path, allowing our biases to be exposed. As the ancient proverb says, "The wisdom of the prudent is to give thought to their ways. The folly of fools is deception." We can't deceive ourselves and still get to our desired goal. The goal of creating space is transformation of our thinking, limiting traits, and unproductive behaviors. The Here-to-There Journey is not about climbing rungs on a ladder in a corporate environment; it is about becoming a leader, the best version of yourself, a person of greater influence in order to help others succeed in life.

The goal of creating space is transformation, which is achieved by developing more productive habits, by letting go of the restrictive and unproductive behavior until the new behavior becomes second nature. To seek truth in the Story not only requires time and truth, but a hunger and humility. It's not easy to pursue truth, especially the higher you go in an organization and when, by nature, we tend to be defensive. We hide.

THE THREE CREATIONS OF LEADERSHIP FOR BREAKTHROUGH PERFORMANCE

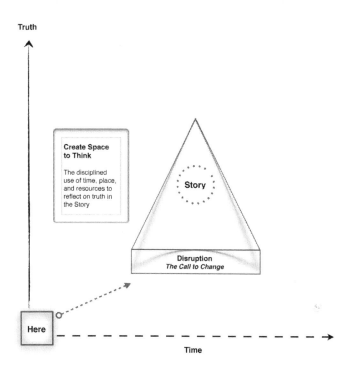

It's not easy to be willing to pursue the truth about our development and our need for growth, which requires maturity, a long journey. As Brené Brown writes in *The Gifts of Imperfection*, "Owning our story can be hard but not nearly as difficult as spending our lives running from it. Embracing our vulnerabilities is risky but not nearly as dangerous as giving up on love and belonging and joy—the experiences that make us the most vulnerable. Only when we are brave enough to explore the darkness, will we discover the infinite power of our light." Truth in the Story brings freedom to move forward, maturing as a person and a leader.

In his book, *The Ideal Team Player*, Patrick Lencioni identifies three virtues of a great team player. The first is *humility*. This is a person who lacks excessive ego or concern with status. The second virtue is *hunger*. People who are always looking for more, and who are growth oriented, are hungry. The third virtue, suggests Lencioni, is street-*smart*. A person with common sense about people, emotional intelligence. Humble, hungry, and smart are key words that describe great team players.

On the way from Here to There, you will encounter disruption, but you have options. Limited though they may be, still you have options. You can keep doing what you've been doing, and hope for a different outcome, or you can create space to think. That's how you discover truth and your options and move from Here to There.

Unselfish Concentration on Self

When people ask me about leadership coaching, I try to describe what can happen in a coaching engagement, what I help my clients experience. First of all, in leadership coaching, we develop a 30,000-foot view. Whether coaching is delivered as one-on-one executive coaching or in a team-based setting, it's about thinking from a new perspective on truth in the Story.

We start out with that 30,000-foot view, but then there's a 10,000-foot view. The 30,000-foot view is the coaching conversations. Next is the personal focus meeting, which compares to a 10,000-foot view. You're closer to it, but you're gaining objectivity; you are able to see some blind spots, because you're reviewing the Story when you're not in the emotion that drives your personal brand of unproductive behavior.

From the 30,000- to the 10,000-foot perspective, the goal is to show up differently in real time. We practice at 30,000 feet by reviewing what's going on in the Story. The goal is to predetermine or *plan* how you will show up differently today. Leaders create space for each level of reflection, in pursuit of truth in the Story and to achieve breakthrough performance.

The Work of Leaders

Creating space to think allows you to evaluate how you spend your time. There are two helpful elements to use when thinking about the workplace experience: *"the job"* and *"the work."* The job is the to-do list, the tasks, the business of everyday busy. *The work* is how you add value to the team. Where do you create value for others, or for the organization? Then the question becomes how much do you work? How much of your workplace experience is spent doing the job?

The majority of people spend 110 percent of their week doing the job and neglecting the work. How much time do you spend in the work each week? Realistically, it depends upon where you are in the organization. If you're a senior leader, it could easily be 40 percent of your time needs to be invested in the work and 60 percent doing the job. It could even be higher, depending on the size of the organization. If you're a senior manager, you could easily spend 20 percent of your time in the work, creating value, and 80 percent doing the job. That means eight hours each week when you're cultivating relationships, coaching, creating space to think, and adding value.

Frontline managers might invest 10 percent of their time on the work and 90 percent of their time doing the job. From a frontline employee, we could expect 3 to 5 percent of their time bringing value to the organization by offering solutions and improvements to their work and 95 percent of their time doing the job.

The Ramifications of Limited Space

What happens if you don't create space? When we don't think, we do the unthinkable. When we're hyper-busy, we get caught up in the whirlwind, so the things that matter most are blown away by the urgent. We keep doing the same thing over and over without results. When we don't pursue the truth in the Story, we buy a lie. We embrace deception and avoidance, which keeps us rooted in Stuckville.

The story of humanity is filled with the response, "I didn't think that would happen" following a poor decision. Why? People don't think. As a next-level leader, you have three responsibilities designed to help you influence others: connect, create, and coach. Let's take a deeper look at these components.

When a leader connects, it's about **discovering the Story**. The question that must be answered is *"What got us Here?"*

To *create* is to **explore the possibilities.** The questions to ask are *"What does There look like? How can you get better?"*

Then to *coach* is to **care for the person.** The questions are *"How will we get there? How can I help you get there?"*

These three C's of next-level leaders align with the research of Richard Boyatzis, and Annie McKee. In their book, *Resonant Leadership*, they identify the three elements required for the hard work of leadership.

The first element is mindfulness, which they define as living in a state of full, conscious awareness of one's whole self, other people, and the context in which we live and work. The key features of mindfulness are (1) attention to what is going on *outside you*, (2) what is going on *inside you*, (3) no judgment!!!, and (4) each moment. This is meant to be done all the time, not just when creating space to reflect. The second element is hope, which enables us to believe that the future we envision is attainable, and to move toward our visions and goals, while also inspiring others toward those goals. A resonant leader would also have the element of compassion, which is the ability to understand people's wants and needs, and to be motivated to act on those feelings.

The need to create space could never be greater. As Boyatzis and McKee concluded, "Leaders today face unprecedented challenges that can result in a vicious cycle of stress, pressure, sacrifice, and dissonance. To counter the inevitable challenges of leadership roles, we need to engage in a *conscious process of renewal*, both on a daily basis and over time. To do so, most of us need to intentionally transform our approach to managing ourselves, and we need to learn new behaviors, practices that enable us to maintain internal resonance and attunement with those we lead." Leaders create space to accomplish this.[17]

How to Create Space

The Story brings conflict, surprise, and emotion, along with the egos involved. That's when we need to **pause and breathe**, which can take alternative forms. To P.A.C.E. yourself could include a daily, thirty-minute personal focus meeting. It could be a decision to reschedule a difficult conversation for another time, or it could be a three-second reset, in real time, to avoid speaking out of emotion or a desire to control.

After a pause, we then can have real-time conversations and engage others in effective communication. In their book, *How to Have That Difficult Conversation You've Been Avoiding*, Henry Cloud and John Townsend identify four fears that push us to avoid conflict and truthful conversations: the fear of (1) losing the relationship, (2) being the object of anger, (3) being hurtful, and (4) being perceived as bad.[18] In their book *Crucial Conversations*, Patterson, Grenny, McMillan, and Switzler define such real-time moments as "crucial conversations."[19] The characteristics of such conversations are that they occur between two or more people, when the stakes are high; opinions vary, emotions run strong, and the topic matters. No wonder we dodge the hard chat.

All of this brings us to the biological support found in **pause and breathe**, to promote positive engagement. We must create a little space if we're not going to be in reactionary mode. Therefore, we can be responsive to engage another.

P.A.C.E. yourself, pause and breathe, and **ask questions**. The intent of asking questions is to engage, not to control. It's to have influence, not to get your way. Once you recognize you're not in control of the other person, you most likely will be in better control of yourself. You can also be in charge without being a control freak. Again, the goal is to have influence. The powerful thing about open-ended questions is that they slow things down. They are so helpful when adrenaline is high and your fight-or-flight mode kicks in, when emotions run strong and something matters, and especially when you're caught by surprise.

Open-ended questions are your new best friend. They must be anchored and precise. To anchor a question involves using a keyword such as How, Who, When, What, or Where to start the question. If you anchor a question with one of those, one of the five W's or How, it almost guarantees that you're going to ask an open-ended question, instead of a leading or a yes-or-no question. If I have a suggestion I want to make, I find anchoring it with "what if" is extremely beneficial. The other W question is Why? (as in, "Why did you do *that*, stupid?"). Add tone and emotional energy, and you have an unproductive, open-ended question.

P.A.C.E. yourself, pause and breathe, ask questions, and **challenge beliefs**. Remember the equation, Ev + B = Em, discussed in an earlier chapter? The *Event* plus what we *Believe* creates an *Emotion*. We need to **challenge our beliefs** because what we believe delivers either a negative reaction or positive response. The event is the event, the person is the person, the situation is the situation, but what you believe about the person or event or situation is what creates the outcome or the emotion. We know that out-of-control emotions usually lead to unproductive behavior. Interestingly, emotions that appear to be completely under control (but suppressed) are even worse.

One way to challenge your beliefs is to ask: "What am I accepting as true?" Followed by, "How do I know that is true?" It's important when you're trying to pace yourself to challenge your beliefs. Don't be afraid to admit it: "There's no way I could really know that." Remember, there's always more to the Story. Jumping to conclusions or making assumptions rarely lead to truth. Asking questions will help you pace yourself.

P.A.C.E. yourself, pause and breathe, ask questions, challenge beliefs, and **edit the Story**. There are two ways in which to do this. There is a forward-looking, future-oriented editing, and there is the historical, the looking back on something that happened in preparation for the next time.

In a coaching session, it's not unusual for a leader to bring a real-world story from the past week. When she does, we often edit that story for the coaching opportunity. I do that by asking these three questions. (1) What happened? (2) What did you want to happen? (3) How would *you* have to show up for that to happen? Asking those three questions allows editing of a story from a historical perspective, so that in the future, it's more likely that the manager can give a positive, productive response, rather than a negative or unproductive response.

When it comes to looking toward the future and editing the Story, there are three questions as well. (1) What got you Here? (2) What does There look like? (3) How will you get There? Creating space to think and to use these questions will produce insights and support the expansion of your influence as a leader, and help you write the Story you want.

The personal focus meeting is the opportunity for you to create space with yourself. It's a disciplined use of time, place, and resources to reflect on truth in the Story. The personal focus meeting is you listening to your Story, pursuing truth in the Story. That's when editing the Story is really helpful. A personal focus meeting is your 10,000-foot view. (We'll explore the personal focus meeting in chapter ten).

One of the challenges I face in coaching leaders is their belief that they don't have time for a daily personal focus meeting. Perhaps you're thinking the same thing, "I'm so busy!" The truth is you don't have time. You must *create space*. It won't just happen; there is a conspiracy, remember? Whenever you want to do something that matters, what do you do to get it done? That's right, you schedule an appointment. Think about the activities that you schedule an appointment for. Whether it's a doctor or dental appointment; or to meet with a financial planner or a therapist; or to get your hair cut or colored; or a round of golf or lunch—when it matters, you schedule an appointment.

So, the question is do you see the benefit of creating space to think? If so, you will have to fight for it, and that starts with your calendar. The thing about an appointment is this, if you don't make an appointment, then you can't keep it, miss it, or reschedule it. And most likely, you'll keep doing the same thing you're doing now. However, if you do schedule an appointment, you have options: you can keep it, cancel it, reschedule it, or yes, ignore it.

My recommendation, as you begin to think about scheduling a personal focus meeting, is to start short and expand as the desire grows. What if you were to schedule ten to fifteen minutes each day? Find a time that you can "shut the door" on the noise and the distraction and the whirlwind, and create space to think, to reflect on the truth in the Story, and consider what's been going on in your life the past twenty-four hours.

It's one thing to improve your thinking; it's another to take action. In the next chapter, we'll explore the second creation of leadership, leading to breakthrough performance.

CREATE SPACE TO THINK

1. How would creating space improve your work as a leader?

2. How much of your day is committed to doing *the job* and how much to *the work*?

3. How will you remember to P.A.C.E. yourself to be more responsive?

Chapter Seven

The Alignment That Creates Clarity

A lack of clarity could put the brakes on any journey to success. It's a lack of clarity that creates chaos and frustration. Those emotions are poison to any living goal.

—STEVE MARABOLI

We must master three creative practices to produce breakthrough performance. In the last chapter, we explored the first, create space to think. When you listen for truth in the Story, this allows you to exercise your ability and willingness to learn and change. The leader's second creation is to *create clarity to act*.

Disruption of your life, schedule, plan, business, even your industry are a given. New obstacles, opportunities, assignments, challenges, and responsibilities are headed your way. You're a leader, and as we discussed in chapter five, the ability to embrace disruption as something that happens *for you* and not *to you* prepares you to take your next Here-to-There Journey.

You expand your influence as a leader when you create space to think, first for yourself, then for others. When you commit time to pursue truth in the Story, the possibility of performance improvement is acknowledged, along with the recognition of what needs to change. Innovation, problem solving, decision making, engaged communication, and finding solutions accelerate for you, your team, and your business. It's easy to be drifting from "I'm so busy" to "I'm too busy." Having no margin and not creating space to think sustains unproductive behavior in your Story, your team's Story, and your company's Story. Remember what happens when we don't think? We do the unthinkable. Growth, productivity, problem solving, innovation, decision making, and breakthrough performance are limited when we don't think.

At the end of a full day, when you drive home, how often do you wonder, "What did I accomplish today? Whose life did I impact in a positive way? How did I make a difference?" When your day is filled with only doing the job (your to-do list and tasks), it's easy to experience a loss of engagement and fulfillment.

We're focused on how to expand your personal influence, how to do more of the work of next-level leaders, how to add value by connecting with people, creating space to think, and coaching them to success, because you care. Such work not only invigorates you, but your team and the business, as well. While you must create space to think and pursue truth in the Story, there is another creative practice to master. You must create clarity to act.

The Hazard of Fog

As twenty-year-old young men, my friend, Ken, and I purchased brand-new Honda motorcycles. In our youthfulness and with a limited cash budget, we bought new 1974 CB360 Honda cycles. We rode our new bikes around Wilson County for the first 1,000 miles to break them in before our big trip.

We planned a road trip from southeast Kansas to southern California. With no windshields and no fear, we traveled up through the Rocky Mountains, down through Reno, Nevada, over to the Pacific Coast Highway, dropping into San Francisco. (I recently read Honda made the bike to ride "around town." It was to be a short-haul machine. Who would like the saddle seat for a long trip? But, we were young.)

Sunburned the first day, we made it to western Kansas. We encountered a hailstorm on our way up to the Rocky Mountains. Imagine the excitement and anticipation of two small-town boys seeing and riding across the Golden Gate Bridge. After an 1,800-mile journey from Neodesha, Kansas, we were ready. Although the bridge is painted international orange for improved visibility, that morning we paid the toll and crossed a bridge we couldn't even see. That's right. The heavy fog made it impossible to take in the bay and the one-and-seven-tenths-mile-long landmark bridge.

Fog is more than a tourist disappointment. According to the U.S. Department of Transportation, fog is a significant weather-related driving hazard. Annually, almost 500 people are killed due to foggy conditions. A traveler's mobility is impacted due to low visibility, requiring reduced speed. Driving in the fog limits visibility and a driver's ability to travel confidently. Fog is hazardous to people on a journey.

Clarity To Get Moving

Every Here-to-There Journey will experience foggy conditions that threaten breakthrough and success. Fog can be a lack of agreement on roles and responsibilities. It can be poorly communicated expectations, a focus on the wrong metrics, or a hectic pace that hinders careful thought and engaged communication. Fog within a team hinders the ability to move easily and productively.

You the know fog is rolling in when purpose is unclear and structure is missing. While you know it's possible to get from Here to There, to achieve your next level, the fog hinders progress. As leaders create space to pursue truth in the Story, the fog lifts, and it's possible to discover a plan to move forward and to improve performance.

The ability and willingness to "scent out the truth" is required to reduce the fog of work. Uncertainty comes when purpose and/or structure are missing. The fog of work is created by a misalignment between purpose and structure and true success. On our diagram of the three creations of leaders, you see the second creation of leaders is to fight the fog by creating clarity.

The Three Creations of Leadership for Breakthrough Performance

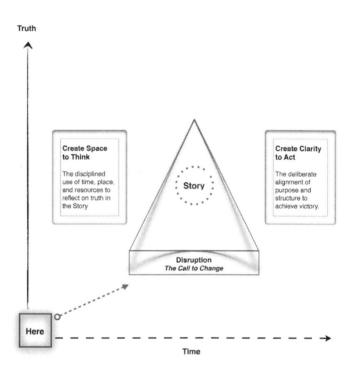

How do we create clarity? First, clarity is the *deliberate alignment of purpose and structure to achieve victory.* Clarity removes uncertainty and helps everyone know what the plan is and what actions to take. Clarity sets us free to leave the safety zone to pursue change when a disruption comes to the Story.

Deliberate Alignment

Creating clarity to act is the *work* of leaders. It's deliberate. You engage a process of change to expand your personal influence. That's leadership development, and it leads to business growth. For a leader who wears his "busy badge," it can be scary to downshift from the adrenaline rush of doing "the job" and living in the whirlwind. However, if you are too busy to slow down and think, then make peace with insanity, uncertainty, a disengaged team, and underperformance.

When it comes to your body and your spine, there are two causes of spinal misalignment. One comes on gradually, due to poor posture, diet, or lifestyle choices. The second results from sudden misalignment due to an accident or injury. I'm working with a fitness trainer, my chiropractor, and a massage therapist to help me correct my posture and the misalignment that creates low back pain and pressure on the nerves in my spine. Like the chiropractor, you must know where there is a lack of alignment. Disruption invites you to identify unproductive behavior, underperformance, resistance, or other obstacles to success. If purpose and structure are not aligned, you will struggle to achieve victory.

Here are a few questions to help you gain insight into the disruption.

- Where do you feel stuck, frustrated, or held back?
- What appears to be hindering your progress or success?
- What's the problem to be solved?
- Where's the resistance to moving forward?
- What must change?
- Where do you need alignment to improve performance?

Creating clarity will improve performance as you deliberately align what needs to be done and why it matters with how to move forward, including a concrete definition of what a win looks like.

Tarnished Silver

When a fine piece of silver is new and unused, it has a shiny, mirrorlike surface. Over time, tarnish develops. Chemistry teacher Ted Beyer explains, "the tarnish is actually the result of a chemical reaction between the silver and sulfur-containing substances in the air. The silver is combining with sulfur and forming silver sulfide. Silver sulfide is black.

When a thin coating of silver sulfide forms on the surface of silver, it darkens the silver."[20]

The beauty of a clear purpose is "tarnished" when the pace of life, lack of reflection, and the noise and distractions of life have dimmed your purpose. It's still there; it just needs to be polished. To create clarity, you must first clean and polish the purpose of a proposed strategy, decision, or change. In the midst of disruption, it's easy to lose sight of "why."

Frustration due to unfulfilled expectations and underperformance can cloud the stabilizing effect of knowing why we need to change, to experience a breakthrough.

Purpose emphasizes the higher reason for alignment in thinking, behavior, and performance: to achieve the goal. To polish the purpose in pursuit of clarity, consider the following questions: What caused the disruption? What's the motivation for this change? Obtaining agreement on the purpose improves buy in, and will guide communication as you build the structure to support the change and achieve a win.

Structure To Execute

A high purpose is not enough to produce a breakthrough performance. To fulfill a purpose requires structure, how you will arrange and organize the team and the work or the project to get moving. How will the plan be carried out? We're talking about execution.

Every living organism has basic structural and functional units called cells. The word "cell" comes from the Latin, "cella," meaning "small room." Each team, department, or division of your company must be structured to allow top performance. A shared purpose unites, but it does not deliver results. Structure describes how your team will work together to get results. Again, we create clarity to act; clarity comes from the deliberate alignment of purpose and structure to achieve victory.

Remember, what got you Here will not get you There. And to keep doing the same thing while expecting a different result is ridiculous. The call of clarity is a call to action, to get moving. Having created space to think and clarity to act, use these questions regarding how to move forward: What are the first steps? How do we organize for execution, communication, and accountability? What needs to happen to support the breakthrough? What are the early wins that lead to the ultimate victory?

The Checkered Flag

Leaders create space and clarity for a reason, to achieve victory. We're after more than kumbaya moments. The goal of the next level and the Here-to-There Journey is to produce success. As a leader on the journey, remember three things. (1) What got me Here will not get me There. (2) While Here is to be celebrated, There is greater, better. And (3) to get There, something must end, or I'll be stuck Here.

Disruption is often required to keep us moving forward. Success is hard work, especially when you realize the determining element is usually leadership, not the technical side of the business. With the conspiracy of busy, all the noise and distractions of the work place, it's important to hear the call for change as a call to action which requires you create clarity.

It is in the context of the Here-to-There Journey that disruption is embraced. The desire to achieve victory requires an answer to the question, "What does There look like?" When the pushback and the resistance come, it helps to remember why you do what you do. To win the battle, set clear expectations, accept personal responsibility for your role, be accountable, and define success. These steps support the hard work of breakthrough performance.

To help you define the win, consider these questions. What does There look like? How will you know when you're successful? How will you know when you've won? What Story do you want to tell down the road? Remember that producing breakthrough performance often involves a series of small victories on the way to the bigger breakthrough.

The Clarity Statement

There's one last step required to create clarity, writing your Statement of Agreement and Plan of Action. This is your opportunity to write a brief statement to summarize your commitment. What's your action plan? Now that you have clarity, now that you've aligned your purpose and structure, what's your commitment that will allow accountability and direction so that you achieve victory?

You've heard the call to change and are willing to engage the process of change. You're ready to create space to think, and to create clarity to act. It's time to explore the third creation of leadership, which is to create the opportunity to get better. But first, grab your pen and journal and reflect on the following questions.

CREATE SPACE TO THINK

1. Where do you feel stuck? Where do you want to get better?
2. Where do you need clarity to get moving toward a breakthrough?

Chapter Eight

The Opportunity
to Get Better

Let's make work better. We should all expect more from work. People spend more hours working than anything else. But for too many, work isn't fulfilling, inspiring, or anything more than a means to an end.

— RE:WORK BY GOOGLE

It's a work in progress. Not too long ago the space was overflowing with Bermuda grass, weeds, and bare spots. The transformation of the dirt to a plot of rich soil that supports growth took a lot of effort. The land was loosened and amended with compost, cultivated to make a perfect seedbed. The success of the vegetable garden begins long before the seeds are sown and plants transplanted.

Imagine such a thriving vegetable garden. It's positioned where it gets plenty of sunshine to increase production. The soil, which is vital to the seed's future as a productive plant with strong roots, is healthy.

The master gardner carefully laid out the rows. The vegetable varieties are arranged by the gardner, who understands which plants work well together and which do not. Notice how the tomato plants are near the onions and peppers. The corn is separated from the potatoes—they're not good neighbors.

The garden flourishes. It's alive and changing, supported by the moisture of timely rain and each sunshiny day. Indeed, the Gardner has created an opportunity for growth and development, which allows each and every plant to produce its contribution. The harvest will be delicious.

The Inspiration to Grow "There"

We've established that as a leader you are responsible to *create space to think* and to *create clarity to act* in support of improving performance. Together these provide **the opportunity to get better.** As a "Master Gardner," you are responsible to *cultivate the environment and the culture that inspires people.* As Simon Sinek, author of *Start with Why,* says, *"If your actions inspire others to dream more, learn more, do more, and become more, you are a leader."* You are the author of your Story and a contributor to the Story of your team, business, or organization.

THE THREE CREATIONS OF LEADERSHIP FOR BREAKTHROUGH PERFORMANCE

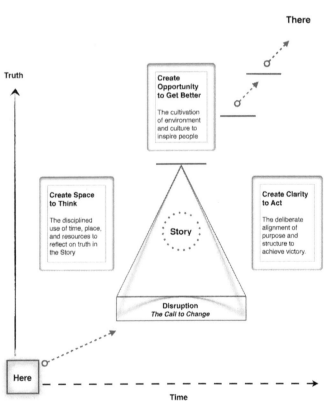

The people you want on your team are committed to becoming their best selves and want to be a part of something significant. They want to flourish, to contribute, to connect their mission to the company's mission. They want to make a difference in the world by using their talents and skills to achieve success and reach their full potential. Like the Master Gardner, it is your work to create opportunities to get better. It is to cultivate a workplace environment and culture that inspires people. A supportive environment (think greenhouse) and a healthy culture (how you roll) are essential if your people and your business are to flourish.

The belief that people want to get better guides us in this work of leaders. As we think about cultivating both the environment and the culture that inspires people, remember the nine observations about business and people introduced in chapter one. I've **highlighted** the ones that speak to the work of leaders.

1. **The business of business is people.** You'll get the technical part of your business, or you won't be in business. Ignore the development of your people, and it will cost you.

2. Business eats people.

3. People don't think.

4. **People need help to become successful people.** While you might think, "People should just show up and do their job," that's not reality.

5. **It takes mature people to develop mature people.** How mature are your behaviors? Your leadership team's behaviors? Your manager's behaviors? Now, what do you expect from your frontline employees, if that is true?

6. **Take care of the people, and the people will take care of the business.** As Gallup reports, "Most workers, many of whom are millennials, approach a role and a company with a highly defined set of expectations. They want their work to have meaning and purpose. They want to use their talents and strengths to do what

they do best, every day. They want to learn and develop. They want their job to fit their life."[21]

7. If you take care of the people and they don't take care of the business, they're not your people.

8. It's supposed to be hard.

9. Everyone wants to be appreciated.

To build a great team, you must recruit the right people, and then, develop, train, and inspire them. Think of your workplace as a garden plot: people are unique contributors who, given a supportive environment, will flourish and be productive. As you cultivate the environment and the culture that inspires people, you will achieve success together.

Engaged, to Be or Not to Be

What, then, are the conditions that affect the growth, health, and progress of people in today's workplace? Consider the eight expectations, identified through Gallup's research, that today's workforce expects:

1. Frequent communication with their manager

2. Development opportunities

3. Flexibility and autonomy

4. Coaching

5. A sense of stability and security

6. To be engaged and motivated

7. Doing work that feels meaningful

8. To make the most of their talents and strengths[22]

This is the opportunity before you. This is how you will win the hearts and the contributions of today's workers. From a macro level, this is your There. Yes, you are at the right place at the right time to make a difference. As a leader who creates space to think and creates clarity to act, you are positioned to create, for your people, the opportunity to get better and produce breakthrough performance. As you see this amazing opportunity, you and your team can build a workplace that attracts and develops the best people to take care of your customers and business.

Flourishing People

The Master Gardner arranges the garden so her fruit-bearing plants experience pollination. She understands each variety, which ones work well together and which do not, to create a plan so the garden flourishes. The word flourish comes from the Latin, "flower." What changes are needed, if your *work* is to create a workplace where people flourish? When people flourish, they experience success, they prosper, they are reaching their next level of development and influence. What does such an environment look like? Let's turn our attention to Gallup's research.

For years, Gallup has provided insight into the workforce, as business leaders wrestle with strategies on how to attract, retain, engage, and improve performance. The *State of the American Workplace* is Gallup's in-depth research, the results of which were first made available in 2010. Their book, *12: The Elements of Great Managing*, provides insight into how we can cultivate the environment and culture that inspires people. Here are the twelve areas, arranged around the four employee needs:

Basic Needs—Level 1

Q01: I know what is expected of me at work.

Q02: I have the materials and equipment I need to do my work right.

Individual Needs—Level 2

Q03: At work, I have the opportunity to do what I do best every day.

Q04: In the last seven days, I have received recognition or praise for doing good. work.

Q05: My supervisor, or someone at work, seems to care about me as a person.

Q06: There is someone at work who encourages my development.

Teamwork Needs—Level 3

Q07: At work, my opinions seem to count.

Q08: The mission or purpose of my company makes me feel my job is important.

Q09: My associates or fellow employees are committed to doing quality work.

Q10: I have a best friend at work.

Growth Needs—Level 4

Q11: In the last six months, someone at work has talked to me about my progress.

Q12: This last year, I have had opportunities at work to learn and grow.[23]

Engage. Inspire. Flourish.

When you create space to *think* and create clarity to act you are more likely to *create the opportunity to get better*, for people to be engaged, inspired, and to flourish. This defines *the work* of a leader and identifies your responsibility and privilege as a next-level leader to cultivate the twelve elements of engagement.

What are the characteristics of engaged people? Gallup's definition defines **engaged** employees as *"highly involved in and enthusiastic about their work and workplace. They are psychological 'owners,' drive performance and innovation, and move the organization forward."*[24]

Engaged people are inspired and free to flourish. The master gardner's work is to provide the environment that allows each plant to grow, to produce, to reach maturity, and bear much fruit. How? By paying attention to the conditions that influence the growth, health, and progress of the plants. When you and your team flourish, your business will also be successful and prosper. Paying attention to the environment you and your team needs to flourish is vital to success.

The other key word is "inspired": engaged people are inspired people. Managers operating as leaders bring the best out of their teams by inspiring, bringing purpose to the business beyond paychecks and profits. The culture—how you roll—meets their engagement needs, so that they put their energy into driving results.

When we don't create the opportunity to get better, if we don't cultivate an environment and culture that inspires people, how can we expect an engaged team? Gallup calls such employees "not engaged." They "are psychologically unattached to their work and company. Because their engagement needs are not being fully met, they're putting time—but not energy or passion—into their work." When you create space to think and create clarity to act, your opportunity to convert the unengaged increases.

Actively disengaged employees aren't "just unhappy at work—they are resentful that their needs aren't being met and are acting out their unhappiness. Every day, these workers potentially undermine what their engaged coworkers accomplish." Remember, if you take care of your people, and they don't take care of your business, then they're not your people. Your only option may be to let them join another organization or business. Again, creating space to think and clarity to act are required to pursue the truth in the Story as you end the relationship with dignity.[25]

Growing Successful People

Henry Cloud, psychologist and author, discusses what it takes to be a successful person when he writes:

> Be oriented toward growth. Growth is natural. Everything alive grows. Things that do not grow are in bad shape. When people are not growing, it is typically because they are afraid of where growth will take them, that it may take them to new and uncomfortable places. People who are oriented toward growth are comfortable with discomfort. They know that initial discomfort will be rewarded with new abilities. The ability

to see the outcome that will be attained through growth is a necessary motivation to get through the difficulties that will be encountered. Growers have the ability to *see the destination* and take in the necessary fuel from the available resources in order to get there.[26]

How oriented toward growth are you? Next-level leaders find fulfillment when they help others achieve more than they thought they could accomplish. Helping others go further, dream bigger, fulfill their purpose, find joy, and be engaged in meaningful work. You know how much of your life you invest at work; why not make it possible for your people and your business or organization to flourish?

With the three creations of leadership identified, let's look at your career Journey to becoming a better boss. But first, it's time to reflect.

CREATE SPACE TO THINK

1. What qualities do you need in order to flourish?
2. How oriented toward growth are you? Why is that?
3. How would you rate your workplace environment on the twelve areas of need for an engaged workforce?

Chapter Nine
The Career Journey

*How you climb a mountain is more
important than reaching the top.*

The Google story begins at Stanford University in 1995, when Larry Page and Sergey Brin stumbled into their partnership with a goal to create a search engine for the World Wide Web. Google, Inc. was officially born in August 1998, with the mission, "To organize the world's information and make it universally accessible and useful." Yes, the primary objective is a continuous search for better answers.

Beginning in a dorm room, then moving to a garage in Menlo Park, California, Google now employs more than 60,000 people in fifty countries, and makes hundreds of products used around the world. Their passion remains to, "Build technology for everyone".

Fast forward to 2009, what could be on the mind of Larry and Sergey? Deep inside the Googleplex, the statisticians were given an assignment code-named, Project Oxygen. According to the New York Times, it involved leadership development. But wait, what could be more important to the future of Google than coming up with a new algorithm or app? The answer—they wanted to build better bosses.[27]

Such a Common Story

How many times have you seen this situation happen? It's called a promotion. The successful *individual* contributor, someone really good in sales for instance, is tapped to become the new sales manager. The team leader. The boss, if you will. Now what? The new manager must prove the company was right, that she is worthy of the trust, the role, the responsibilities. That she became successful knowing the answers and getting the job done as an individual contributor is a given. No one delivered the message: "What got her Here won't get her There." She moves into her new office and installs a "Please take a number" system outside the door. The deception of command and control is not an issue of generation or gender only, and it will likely disengage the top talent, slow the decision-making process, and limit innovation and collaboration, until finally the sales department begins to stall out, and she becomes another casualty.

Fantastic individual performers are often promoted to manager without the support and development of skills necessary to lead. The ability to do the work, if you will. Believing that the business of business is people, that when a company takes care of the people and selects the right people, those people will take care of the business. For the new manager to expand her influence, she must move from high expertise to the ability to influence others, to get work done with and through others.

Leader or Manager?

When I speak on change and the Here-to-There Journey, I often ask my audience two questions. One, "How many of you want to be managed?" Very few hands go up. Then I ask the second question, which is, "How many of you want to be influenced?" Nearly every hand goes up. To further drive the point home, I ask one last question, "How many of you would welcome a leader in your life who knows and understands you, knows your strengths and weaknesses, your hopes and dreams, believes in you, wants what is best for you, and wants to help you succeed?" Virtually all hands are up, and some people are putting both hands up. That's how hungry people are for a next-level leader.

Managers oversee projects, sales, budgets, and production processes. They manage the job. Great leaders release control, while accepting the responsibility of being in charge. They set out to lead, to influence the team, and achieve greater success. Leaders create space to think, first for themselves and then, for others. To create space is to be intentional and disciplined in your use of time, place, and resources, to seek and reflect on truth in the Story.

Contrast the Focus of Managers and Leaders

People are open to influence, but resistant to attempts to control or manage them. Remember what happens when I ask an audience, "How many of you would embrace the influence of someone who knows you, understands your strengths and weaknesses, only wants what is best for you, and can help you win?" Hands go up all over the room. Why? Consider this list of differences between a manager and a leader:

- Managers seek control. Leaders are in charge and have influence.
- Managers want to be the go-to person. Leaders collaborate and delegate for execution.
- Managers give answers. Leaders ask open-ended questions.
- Managers see people as cogs in the machine. Leaders see the people and their potential, and are there to serve.
- Managers dictate the plan. Leaders cast a vision.
- Managers blame the people. Leaders accept responsibility.
- Managers develop subordinates. Leaders develop other leaders.
- Managers live in the whirlwind. Leaders create space.
- Managers do the job. Leaders do the work.

The Eight Habits of Google Managers

What do you believe it takes to be a manager? Laszlo Bock, Google's vice president of people operations, Google's human resources department, admitted they had it wrong. "In the Google context, we'd always believed that to be a manager, particularly on the engineering side, you need to be as deep or deeper a technical expert than the people who work for you." Mr. Bock continued, "It turns out that that's absolutely the least important thing. It's important, but pales in comparison. Much more important is just making that connection, and being accessible."[28]

Google took the deep dive into the data gathering, and reviewed thousands of observations about managers, performance reviews, and feedback surveys, then encoded the comments looking for patterns. While credit is given Google's team, the list reinforces what we know to be true. The eight habits of highly effective Google managers are listed below.

1. Be a good coach. Provide feedback and have regular one-on-one meetings with your team.

2. Empower your team and don't micromanage. Give freedom while being a resource.

3. Express interest in employee success and well-being. See the people as people.

4. Be productive and results oriented. Set expectations and help the team win, prioritizing the work and making decisions to keep things moving.

5. Be a good communicator and listen to your team. That's about engaged communication. Listen and share. Focus on the team result.

6. Help your employees with career development.

7. Have a clear vision and strategy for the team, meaning to keep focused on goals and strategy, then progress.

8. Have key technical skills so you can advise. Don't take over, but be able to contribute to the work when needed.[29]

What about the Work?

As management consultant and author Margaret Wheatley writes, "For me, this is a familiar image. People in the organization ready and willing to do good work, wanting to contribute their ideas, ready to take responsibility, and leaders are holding them back, insisting that they wait for decisions or instructions."[30] One responsibility of the leading manager is to clear the path, so her team can do the job.

Every employee from the front lines to the CEO has incorporated in his or her role and responsibility both "the work" and "the job." When I make this distinction, this is what I mean. The job includes tasks, to-do lists, the stuff that keeps you busy and causes your adrenaline to rush and your stress to increase. Conflict is to be expected and can be healthy, when properly engaged. But when there's a lack of connection, little time to think, and limited coaching, the survival fight-or-flight instinct kicks in. As a leader, it's easy to overlook the issues that affect your team when your time, focus, and energy is consumed by the job.

When it comes to the work, the work is the time and energy dedicated to adding value. The purpose of a leader is to create value beyond investment of time doing the job. How do you create value? Of course, it begins by creating space to think. First for yourself, and then for others. You create value by keeping the vision alive, and noticing what's going on in the organization, your industry, and the next disruptor. A leader identifies challenges and opportunities.

The leader creates value by creating clarity, that intentional alignment of purpose and structure that leads to victory. When you create space to think, you develop an environment where innovation can take place. Problem solving happens, and decisions get made. That's adding value. When you're doing the work, you're creating a culture that values influence, productive behavior, and performance improvement. It builds on the foundation of trust. Experience is effective communication. The culture secures commitment from the team, provides accountability to support success, and focuses on team results. That is how you create value.

Before we turn our attention to the structure that brings focus to your organization, I invite you to think about your career journey, or perhaps what you want for the emerging leaders in your business.

CREATE SPACE TO THINK

1. What are your thoughts on managing people vs. leading people?

2. Manager or leader behaviors—which best describe your style?

3. When you revisit the eight qualities of boss at Google, how would you rate yourself on each habit?

Part Three:

The Structure of Focused Time

Chapter Ten

The Personal Focus Meeting

Follow effective action with quiet reflection. From the quiet reflection will come even more effective action.
— PETER DRUCKER

"Breathe in through your nose, exhale out your mouth," my personal trainer reminds me.

This time I was finishing my one-hour workout on the rowing machine. Ashley set my goal. "I want you to row 250 meters. You'll repeat this three times. Following a brief recovery time, I want you to beat your previous time." If you're unfamiliar, rowing works nearly all your muscles from your shoulders to your calves. It's a full-body and cardio exercise. They say you can burn up to 50 percent more calories. The rowing machine takes a lot of concentration for me to breathe correctly.

Round one: One minute and six seconds. Round two: One minute and two seconds. "Remember the goal to beat your previous time," Ashley challenges me. Round three: Fifty-eight seconds. I'm winded. She reminds me, "Breathe in through your nose, exhale out your mouth."

"Why . . . in the nose . . . out . . . the mouth?" I question, struggling to catch my breath.

"It's calming. When you inhale through your nose, it helps slow your heart down and aids your recovery time," she answers. "Breathing through your mouth delays your recovery."

The rowing machine reminds me of life and the workplace. The pace is fast, "do more with less." There's resistance. It's breathtaking, hard work, and rewarding. Learning to create space supports your results and recovery. Disruption comes, calling your name and demanding change. To respond, leaders create space through the disciplined use of time, place, and resources to pursue truth in the Story. And tucked away in the word "space" is the secret answer to how you will not only recover, but enjoy breakthrough performance. To create space in the midst of conflict and the daily challenges of life and work, learn to P.A.C.E. yourself, pause, and breathe. Ask questions. Challenge your beliefs and edit the Story. To create space, clarity, and change, you must commit to your Personal Focus Meeting. Remember, leaders create space to think, first for themselves.

The Genesis of Breakthroughs

A Personal Focus Meeting (PFM) is a meeting focused on you. It's you with you and the Story. It's your opportunity to pursue truth in the Story and to think, reflect, inquire, and listen. While your PFM includes time to focus on the people you lead and the business you manage, it is first about your personal growth and leadership development. The PFM becomes your 30,000-foot view of the Story. You step out of the whirlwind, the busyness of the job, the noise and distractions to do the foundational part of your work as a leader—thinking. It's time to connect the dots, gain perspective, and hold yourself accountable for your contribution, your role and responsibilities, and your commitments and goals. You get to put your busy badge in the drawer for fifteen, thirty, sixty minutes of created space to think, so that you write the Story you want to tell. Fewer regrets. More influence.

It's an Appointment

The Personal Focus Meeting is a commitment of you, to you. Like coaching and leadership development, it is unselfish concentration on self to serve others, to change unproductive behavior, and get better.

When something matters and you want to make sure it happens, what do you do? That's right, schedule an appointment. Because if it matters, you must schedule and guard the time as if your life depends on it. Because "busy" wants to steal it. Remember "The Conspiracy"?

The PFM is a fundamental commitment of your next-level leadership adventure. Your Here-to-There Journey. The PFM is space that you must create. It's a rare workplace where the expectation is that you *shut the door* on the noise, the distractions, the chaos, to reflect and pursue Truth, also known as feedback, experience, success, and failure. But I urge you to go for it.

The Pen or the Keyboard?

Remember how Ashley encouraged me to inhale through my nose and exhale through my mouth? Taking pen and paper is like breathing in. Not "taking a breath," but more like receiving the benefits of effective breathing to help slow things down. Research by Pam Mueller and Daniel Oppenheimer suggests there are advantages associated with handwritten notes:

> The present research suggests that even when laptops are used solely to take notes, they may still be impairing learning because their use results in shallower processing. In three studies, we found that students who took notes on laptops performed worse on conceptual questions than students who took notes longhand. We showed that, whereas taking more notes can be beneficial, laptop note-takers' tendency to transcribe lectures verbatim, rather than processing information and reframing it in their own words, is detrimental to learning.[31]

Cindi May, reporting on the research in *Scientific American,* notes:

> Students who write out their notes on paper actually learn more. Those students who wrote out their notes by hand had a stronger conceptual understanding, and were more successful in applying and integrating the material than those who took notes with their laptops. Writing by hand is slower and more

cumbersome than typing, and students cannot possibly write down every word in a lecture. Instead, they listen, digest, and summarize so that they can succinctly capture the essence of the information. Thus, taking notes by hand forces the brain to engage in some heavy "mental lifting" and these efforts foster comprehension and retention.[32]

Why do leaders create space, again? Well, if the objective is to have time and a place to slow down and breathe, then an open mind regarding keeping a journal makes sense. Writing in a journal is a discipline, a skill to be learned, and a tool to be used.

A Neglected Discipline

Setting an appointment for reflective thinking and writing is a neglected discipline. By discipline, I mean a systematic method that allows you to succeed in this area of your life. From my experience, there are several reasons this discipline is neglected. Which of the following apply to you? The pace of life—who has time to sit down and write, to think, to ponder, and to listen? Fear—what if someone reads what I write? Worse—what if I discover something about myself I don't want to acknowledge? Skill— how do I move beyond keeping a diary? Value—it's not a priority.

Benefits of Journal Writing

From my perspective, there are four benefits to the discipline of journal writing. The first is it's an inside-out focus, meaning as you capture on paper what is going on inside your busy mind, it quiets the voices and allows you to listen for truth in the Story. Another benefit is focus; all that self-talk and internal chatter makes it difficult to hear. Writing creates space, leading to teachable moments. Perspective is a third benefit to hand writing over using a laptop. Have you ever written a letter just to vent and then trashed it, once you read it? Then you get the point regarding perspective. A final benefit to journaling is legacy. A journal is a private chronicle of your life journey.

Getting Started

For your PFM, here's a little bit of structure to help you get started. First, remember that the truth is in the Story, so we begin your PFM appointment with the headlines in the Story. There are four headlines to consider. *Emotion* is the first headline. As you come to your PFM, what word best describes how you feel right now, and why do you feel that way? The second headline is *gratitude*. What are you thankful for? Who do you appreciate? The third is *celebrate*. Who do you want to recognize, acknowledge, or honor? And the fourth headline is *challenge*. Where is the disruption, frustration, or opposition? Where might you feel stuck? Where do you want or need clarity?

Having checked your Story, there's the possibility of bringing order to your day, because if you don't bring order to it, someone else will. For this discipline, we have a daily planner; it's a three-by-three-by-three daily planner. And with this, you take time to choose the three **goals** that you want to focus on, whether it's for a month, a quarter, six months, or a year. The goal is to answer the questions: What do you want to achieve? What does "There" look like in your current Here-to-There Journey? Is it SMART— *specific, measurable, attainable, relevant, time-bound?* Bullet point your three goals.

In your PFM, go now to your **function**. Function deals with what you're responsible for, based on your role in the organization. How do you serve others in pursuit of your goals? What are the primary duties of your position? What are you responsible for in your role? How do you make a difference in your world?

So we have three goals and three functions, and here's where the day gains order. It's the three **priorities**. What activity needs to be done first, today? What are the most important, nonurgent things you must do today to have a productive day? When I talk about having three priorities, clearly there's more work to do than three things on any given day. So, I suggest a way to prioritize is to think as if you were leaving on vacation at noon today. What would be the three things you must accomplish before leaving town? Those are your three priorities. Planning three by three by three—reminding yourself of your goals, what your role-based functions are, and then your priorities for the day—is a way to stay focused and organized.

Tips for Getting Started

Let me suggest three tips for getting started with your Personal Focus Meeting. First, you must schedule your Personal Focus Meeting as an appointment, even if it's just five minutes. Though, don't be surprised when you start to desire more time. Second, if possible, find a place where you can close the door and minimize any distractions. This means mute the phone, don't look at the computer screen, and turn off the TV, radio, and anything else that can interfere. Clear your mind, because this reflective exercise requires concentration. You can begin to clear your mind by journaling, with your headline check-in. Finally, resources include the Story. What happened yesterday? What happened since the last time you sat down for your PFM? What's going on in the Story, or in the lives of people that you are interacting with? What books are you reading? Have you listened to a TED Talk or podcast that speaks your language? Do you have blogs that are meaningful, that support your personal growth and professional development?

Headline Check-in

1) **Emotion**: What word best describes how you **feel** right now? Because?

2) **Gratitude**: **What** are you thankful for? Or, **who** do you appreciate?

3) **Celebrate**: **Who** do you want to recognize, acknowledge or honor?

4) **Challenge**: Where's the **disruption**, frustration, opposition, conflict? Where did you fail last week? Where do you need/want **clarity**?

How to Open up and Engage the Story

When it comes to listening for truth in the Story, there are two sets of questions that you can use either to edit the Story or to gain clarity for writing the Story. Let's deal first with those questions to edit the Story.

Assume you are reviewing your day yesterday. You had a situation that did not go as you had planned in a relationship, and a conflict occurred. If you want to edit that Story, the first question to ask is what happened? The second question is what did I want to have happen? And then, the third question is how would I show up for that to happen? Please notice that the emphasis is on how you would show up, how *you* would need to change, for a different outcome in that Story.

The second set of three questions is designed to help create clarity for writing the Story that you want to tell. It's more future oriented. The first question is what got me Here? The second, what does "There" look like? And the third question is how will I get There?

Create Space—the Journal

The goal of writing in your journal is to create space for consistent reflection on the truth found in your Story. This discipline of reflective writing moves the internal conversation to the written page. Journal writing promotes the opportunity to think, listen, and when a habit, it will accelerate your personal growth. Here are three steps to help you get started with your PFM and using a journal for your growth.

STEP 1. I recommend using three pens to help bring clarity to the words that you're writing. The first uses black ink, and it is *your voice to you*. This voice captures the Story's context. It's the historical information. It brings perspective, details, and context. It answers the question: What's happened in the Story since your last journal entry? If you write only using black ink, your voice to you, it could be a diary.

STEP 2. Green ink is your *voice in reflection*. Here, you can cultivate a positive outlook and mindset toward life. It's a place to wrestle with and seek clarity, answers, focus, and realignment. Here are a few other questions to use to be reflective in your writing. What is weighing heavily on you right now? Where do you need clarity? Where are you experiencing conflict in your relationships? What expectations are unfulfilled? What's the effect of the unfulfilled expectation? How are you living with purpose and passion? How do you want to show up differently? In the past twenty-four hours, what was the biggest obstacle to your personal success?

Step 3. Red ink is your *next-level leader*, the "other voice" from outside yourself. Now you're ready for active listening, meditation, personal-focus time. You've created space to listen, to capture insights, to discover the truth, and receive directions, solutions, or creative possibilities. The idea is to listen for the other voice that knows you, cares about you and your success, speaks truth to you, is a trusted authority in your life, and only wants what's best for you. This will take some practice, experimenting until you can hear this "other voice." The focus is your next-level Journey. How are you showing up as a leader and doing the work of a leader? You may find your red pen flowing as you capture meaningful quotes and thoughts from your reading of other thought leaders. You can prepare yourself to listen by writing this question, "What would you say to me?" I find it helpful to encourage people to write in the first person, just as if your next-level leader, that other voice, is speaking directly to you. Be sure to listen for affirmation and encouragement as well as correction.

Invite a Guest

Tapping into experts with a lifetime of learning about one subject is another way to begin to hear truth that you wouldn't hear by yourself. So who will teach you? What books are you going to read? What authors speak your language? What podcasts invigorate you? What blogs do you read that are meaningful, helpful to stirring up you as a leader? What books are in your personal library? Ben Franklin is noted to have said, "This library afforded me the means of improvement by constant study, for which I set apart an hour or two each day, and thus repaired in some degree the loss of the learned education my father once intended for me."[33] In our hectic, distracted pace of life, having Personal Focus

Meeting time and reading and listening to helpful, instructive material is one way that you can become a better leader. Part of the reason is when you write you can see more clearly what's going on and whether you're making progress toward writing the Story you want to tell.

The PFM creates space for yourself. What about your influence with others? Before looking at the individual focus meeting, how would you answer the following questions?

CREATE SPACE TO THINK

1. What do you believe about writing in a journal for personal development?
2. When could you schedule ten to fifteen minutes for reflection?
3. Who would you invite to your PFM?

Get more resources and templates at
LeadersCreateSpace.com.

Chapter Eleven
Individual Focus Meeting

Performance is either improved or diminished
by the other people in your scenario.
—Henry Cloud

We systematically overestimate the value of access to information and
underestimate the value of access to each other.
—Clay Shirky

What really releases energy is the personal attention you give to
helping people leverage and grow their talents.
—Ram Charan

The hotel ballroom is filled with American Airline's management team, the leadership team responsible for getting the job done with and through others. Their task, as always, is performance improvement and getting positive results in a beleaguered industry. "In the military, they give medals to people who are willing to sacrifice themselves so that others may gain," Simon Sinek says, from the front of the enormous room. Long pause. "In business, we give bonuses to people who are willing to sacrifice others so that we may gain." Pin-dropping silence. "What message must you communicate as a leader?" he asks. "I've got your back." He continues speaking as if addressing a valued team member. "There is nothing you can break that I can't help put back together. I believe in you even when you no longer believe in yourself." Sinek is a marketing consultant, author, and motivational speaker.

During the Q and A session, someone stands in the back of the room and asks, "How can I get the most out of my people?" "You need more empathy," he replies. After making it clear she has asked the wrong question, he continues, "You need to take the time to find out what they need to do their job better. You need to be asking, 'What can I do to help?'" To end the two-hour interaction, he advocates for the true test of leadership. "When you ask someone how they're doing . . . " He waits, and the room quiets with another extended pause. *"Do you actually care?"* Leaders create space first for themselves and then for others. In this chapter, we will explore the individual focus meeting, an IFM, quite often a missing discipline of the leader's work.

Beyond the Shareholder

Simon Sinek has dedicated his life to undoing what he believes General Electric's CEO, Jack Welch, did to business. Sinek argues, "Beginning in the 1980s, more and more businesses started using humans to balance the books." He observes how Welch was "notorious for the intense pressure he put on employees to perform at all cost. Anyone perceived to be underperforming was fired. And when profits dropped, there were mass layoffs." Indeed, the corporate structure that emerged was to "maximize shareholder profit." Sinek's vision, in contrast to Welch's goal, is to "create a world in which the vast majority of people wake up every single morning inspired to go to work, feel safe when they're there, and return home fulfilled at the end of the day."[34]

No One Succeeds Alone

Clinical psychologist Henry Cloud, in his book, *The Power of the Other,* contends that no great leader succeeds alone. Everyone needs trustworthy connections with people who will listen to problems, sympathize, offer honest feedback, and provide support, respect, and accountability. Dr. Cloud emphasizes the importance of overcoming isolationist self-reliance in favor of developing supportive, positive relationships that contribute to our well-being and success. The IFM, a meeting focused on an individual, is part of the structure that supports next-level performance, so people are inspired, feel safe, and are fulfilled. As Dr. Cloud accurately points out, "So called self-improvement, the process of getting better, is really a *relational* enterprise, not a self-enterprise."[35] It takes mature people to develop mature people.

Relationships Matter

Consider that some of the most influential people in history had mentors. The following list includes just a few high achievers who had people of influence in their lives: Maya Angelou, mentor to Oprah Winfrey. Benjamin Mays, mentor to Martin Luther King, Jr. Steve Jobs, mentor to Mark Zuckerberg. Woody Guthrie, mentor to Bob Dylan. Larry Summers, mentor to Sheryl Sandberg. Father Michael van der Peet, mentor to Mother Teresa. Katie Russell, mentor to and mother of NBA star Bill Russell. Luther Powell, mentor to and father of Colin Powell. Harford Steele, high school civics teacher, mentor to John Glenn.

Notice how many of the mentors are known for their influence in the lives of the superachievers. A high school teacher, a pastor, a mother, a father. Whose life will you influence, perhaps supporting their success beyond what you will achieve? John Maxwell says it well, "Great partnerships make you better than you are. They multiply your values, enable you to do what you do best, allow you to help others do their best, give you more time, help you fulfill the desires of your heart, and compound your vision and effort."[36]

Why Would They Leave?

Google's "Project Oxygen" started with three basic assumptions regarding why people leave a company. One, they lack connection to the mission of the company or a belief that their work matters. Two, they don't like or respect their coworkers. Three, they have a terrible boss, which is what got Google's attention. The impact on employees' performance and how they felt about their job was significantly influenced by the manager. "The starting point was that our best managers have teams that perform better, are retained better, are happier. They do everything better," Laszlo Bock, Google's vice president of people operations says. "So the biggest controllable factor that we could see was the quality of the manager and how they sort of made things happen. The question we then asked was, 'What if every manager was that good?' And then you start saying, 'Well, what makes them that good and how do you do it?'"

What Makes for an Effective Leader?

In chapter eight, we looked at the eight habits of effective managers in Google's world. It happens to be a great list for most, if not all, managers who want to lead people. Here's Google's list of eight habits of highly effective managers to remind you. One, be a good coach. Two, empower your team and don't micromanage. Three, express interest in employees' success and well-being. Four, be productive and results oriented. Five, be a good communicator and listen to your team. Six, help your employees with career development. Seven, have a clear vision and strategy for the team. And last, have key technical skills so you can help advise the team.

What does "be a good coach" mean? Provide specific constructive feedback, balance the negative and the positive comments, and have regular one-on-ones, presenting solutions to problems tailored to the employee's strengths. "You don't actually need to change who the person is," Mr. Bock says. "What it means is if I am a manager and want to get better and I want more out of my people and I want them to be happier, two of the most important things I can do is just make sure I have some *time for them* and to be *consistent*, and that's more important than doing the rest of the stuff."[37]

The Work of Leaders

If you do the job, your time is consumed with to-do lists, the stuff that keeps you busy. It's easy to start seeing the people as cogs in the machine when you're busy doing the job. Conflict is to be expected and can be healthy when properly engaged. But when there is a lack of connection and little time to think, the survival instinct kicks in. As a leader, it's easy to overlook the issues that affect the team when your time, focus, and energy is consumed by doing "the job." However, the work of a leader is what you do to add value—beyond doing the job—to the organization. Your development as a leader falls into this category. We call it your personal focus meeting—when you create space to think about how to get better as a leader, exercising your ability and willingness to learn and change to pursue truth in the Story. The work of leaders also places a high priority on hosting the IFM with each direct report.

The general purpose of the IFM is summed up with the three C's of next-level leaders mentioned in chapter eight. The first C is to connect, which means we discover the Story. The question is what got us Here? The second C is to create space, where we explore the possibilities. The question is what does There look like? And the third C is to coach. The goal is to care about the person, and the question is how will *we* get There?

The Simple Structure

So, if you choose to create space for your direct reports, how do you structure an individual focus meeting? First, you want to capture the context. At the top of the form, there's the employee's name and space to note personality style. (It's where I write the employee's Everything DiSC Workplace style .) Add the location, date, and time of the IFM. The first section is "The Headline Check-In." There are four headlines, from their story, which the employee provides. The first one is **emotion**. The question is what word best describes how you feel right now? Because? The second headline is **gratitude**. What are you thankful for or whom do you appreciate? The third headline is **celebrate**. Whom do you want to recognize, acknowledge, or honor today? The fourth headline is **challenge**. Where is the disruption, frustration, opposition? Where do you feel stuck? Where do you want or need clarity?

Notice the progression: you move from emotion to gratitude to celebration to challenge. And as you do, your direct report—the person you're hosting this IFM for—moves from a self-check (cues you in, too) to a place of gratitude for gifts received. The outward focus continues by looking for someone you catch doing something right. The question, "who do you want to recognize today?" also gives the leader hosting the IFM information about what's going on in the reporter's team that he may not be aware of. The host can pass on his praise and appreciation to that employee as well.

Now, it's time for the challenge: what's going on in their work? And how you can help? This usually opens a coaching conversation about your direct report's leadership, a business challenge, or both.

The second major section of the individual focus meeting is "Big Rocks." The first of these involves their people, their team, succession planning, performance of individual players. The second involves business fundamentals, how are they expanding their personal influence in the business?, What are they focused on changing? This also is a chance for you learn what your direct report needs to be successful by asking, "How can I help?" What activities are they accountable for that move the business to achieve agreed-upon goals?

Remember, it's the employee's individual focus meeting. You are creating space to think, to give and receive feedback, to bounce ideas off one another, to seek your counsel, to collaborate, to be responsible, and to be accountable for expectations of the employee's role on your team. However, it is also a time to ask about things that are on your radar. The "Remember to ask about" section on the form is where you can bullet point anything that's on your mind as it relates to your direct report's performance as you prepare for the meeting. In a cadence of weekly IFMs, it's easier to give time to process an idea, to create a solution, to explore possibilities; the section "Table for next IFM" serves this purpose. It's a place to bookmark ideas that are in process so that you don't forget them.

Then the third and last major section of the IFM agenda is "The Wrap." The W.R.A.P. is an acrostic that stands for four things. The W stands for What—What is your leadership development focus this week? What will be different because of your influence? The R stands for Remember—How will you remember your leadership development commitment? A stands for Action—What's your action plan? What are you responsible for? What are you going to do? And then, P stands for Promise—How will this action plan help you get there? How will it help you and your team reach your goal, improve performance, or achieve team results?

The second part of the W.R.A.P. reviews their business development focus or commitments to move their part of the business. There is room to write one, two, or three goals along with actions that will be done the next week to help achieve the goal.

To manage the weekly IFM, you'll want to have a three-ring binder identified with your direct report's name, in which to store the weekly IFM forms. You then have a chronology telling that employee's Story, work, and performance. This is actually better than an annual performance appraisal, because of weekly or biweekly conversations.

How to Get it Done

The first thing to do is to schedule the appointment. I would suggest that you allow forty-five minutes to an hour for the IFM, depending on the role and responsibility of your direct report. My recommendation is that you meet weekly for the IFM with managers who lead a team with direct reports, and biweekly with frontline managers who deal directly with frontline employees. Treat the IFM as "sacred time" and don't underestimate the value of one-on-one contact with you. Your direct reports want and need time with you. This is dedicated time to connect, create space, and coach. It must be a priority for you to send them the right message and move the business. Hosting the IFM is one of the most important commitments you make in your work as a leader.

The Strong Workplace

The Gallup organization identified twelve characteristics of a strong workplace based on in-depth interviews with more than 80,000 managers from all sizes of companies and all levels of responsibility. Authors Buckingham and Coffman reported the findings in their classic book, *First Break All the Rules*.

Here are the twelve rules written as questions. The more you and/or your direct report can answer "yes," the more likely that employee is engaged.

1. Do I know what is expected of me at work?
2. Do I have the equipment and material I need to do my work?

3. At work, do I have the opportunity to do what I do best every day?

4. In the last seven days, have I received recognition or praise for good work?

5. Does my supervisor or someone at work seem to care about me as a person?

6. Is there someone at work who encourages my development?

7. At work, do my opinions seem to count?

8. Does the mission/purpose of my company make me feel like my work is important?

9. Are my coworkers committed to doing quality work?

10. Do I have a best friend at work?

11. In the last six months, have I talked to someone about my progress?

12. This last year, have I had opportunities at work to learn and grow?[38]

Notice how the IFM supports the creation of a strong workplace as described in this list. The individual focus meeting allows managers to connect, create space, and coach their direct reports and supports these twelve qualities of an engaging workplace. How would you or your team respond to these twelve strengths? How many times would the answer be "yes"?

The Energy of Connection

The IFM builds relationships and creates what Henry Cloud calls, "The Energy of Connection." "Through support, challenge, confrontation, accountability, dealing with failure, loss and pain, observing our performance and giving actionable feedback, relationship imparts the energy of connection to get to the next level."[39] In a healthy culture, the IFM allows a manager to embrace her team while helping them get better. This is the work of leaders and leads to top performance. Leaders create space to build relationships and develop other leaders.

The Millennial-Friendly Workplace

Nearly 75 percent of the workforce will be millennials by 2030. According to a *recent* Forbes article, "Millennials In The Workplace: They Don't Need Trophies But They Want Reinforcement," it may not be about trophies for them after all. What does the relationship between employer and employee look like? There are four concerns of millennials mentioned in this article. First, they want to grow, even if that means growing out of your company. Second, they want a coach, not a boss. They want to know how they're doing. " According to a recent survey conducted by TriNet, a company dedicated to providing HR solutions, 69 percent of millennials see their company's review process as flawed." A major reason for this is the *lack of feedback throughout the year.* The survey also found that three out of four millennials feel "in the dark" about their performance, and nearly 90 percent would feel more confident if they had ongoing check-ins with their boss. "The more frequent the check-ins are, the better," said Rob Hernandez, perform product manager at TriNet. "The biggest issue with the annual review process is the formality. There is often more emphasis on reflection than opportunities for improvement in the future." The third thing millennial employees seek is not to waste time on the little things. The fourth is to have balance and democracy.[40]

There's nothing new here, folks. Millennials want to work with you, not for you. They want to be influenced, not managed. Who doesn't want that in their workplace relationship? Once again, the effective and disciplined use of the IFM is a solid solution. As Henry Cloud puts it, "Science has shown that we can change. We do change. We do get better, but we tend to do it alongside people who believe that too and who are committed to helping us."[41] And of course, that's what the IFM is about.

We've seen how structured focus times for yourself and with your direct reports create the opportunity to get better. Next we see how the focused time with a team works. But first, what are your thoughts?

CREATE SPACE TO THINK

1. How well do you connect with your direct reports? With your supervisor?

2. How important are relationships in your workplace?

3. Why do you think regular check-ins are more effective than performance reviews?

Get more resources and templates at
LeadersCreateSpace.com.

Chapter Twelve
The Team Focus Meeting

Team is not a group of people who work together. A team is a group of people who trust each other.

Not finance. Not strategy. Not technology. It is teamwork that remains the ultimate competitive advantage, both because it is so powerful and so rare.

—Patrick Lencioni

In 2005, I was selected, along with seventeen other managers, to participate in the Cox Executive Leadership Program. At that time, there were 80,000 employees in Cox Enterprises and twenty people were selected each year as part of the leadership development program. That year, two of us were selected from Cox Radio. The twelve-month program included working with an executive coach, a three-night backpacking experience with Outward Bound, and two weeks at corporate.

In April 2005, we came together in North Carolina at Pisgah National Forest on the Blue Ridge Parkway for our excursion into the Linville Gorge (think smaller version of the Grand Canyon). It was a tremendous experience. On the flight home, I captured in my journal my five lessons from the experience.

Lessons from the Wilderness

Lesson one: The Foundation of Trust

Building trust began immediately. In preparation, I purchased all the gear and clothing on the list they gave us. Upon arrival at the site, our guides had us unpack our suitcases. I proudly arranged my stuff on the ground. Their goal was to eliminate as much as possible. "Remember," our guide said, "you're going to carry everything you take these next three days." He continued, "Do you really need an extra pair of underwear? That shirt and those socks?" Several items, previously deemed necessary, became baggage to be left behind.

Trusting our guides continued that first day. They taught us to read a topographical map. After making our first summit, we bushwhacked our way to a target location seen only on the map in the wilderness. I remember finally arriving at a clearing and thinking, "Oh, what a perfect place to set up camp." It was getting dark. And after a brief rest, the guide said, "Well, we really need to keep moving and set up camp near water." I was ready to be done. We resumed hiking into the night. I recall putting one foot after another. I was not in charge; I was the **follower** in this leadership development experience.

Lesson two: The Power of Focus

This lesson was presented during my rappelling experience. I wanted to be one of the first at the top so I wouldn't have to wait too long, totally out of my comfort zone. Good news, bad news. I wasn't first, so I got the opportunity to sit and look out over the Linville Gorge. It was a huge picture-window view, just a beautiful sight. Until the time came to go harness off and do the rappel. Did I mention I have a lot of respect for heights? Did I mention I've never rappelled before and I was totally out of my comfort zone?

The guide talked about the workload of the rope, how it was rated at 1,500 pounds, how the buckles all worked, how to harness in, and how nothing could happen. Finally, the time came to back the edge and rappel. All I could do was focus on what was in front of me to get started down the wall. About half-way down, someone yelled, "Hey, look around." Yes, I was so intent on the task that I was forgetting the journey. That's the power of focus.

Lesson three: The Necessity of Risk

I had to leave the comfort zone of my corner office if I was going to go for it. I had to accept the invitation and show up to participate. I had to leave the staging area, step into the safety zone, and harness up. I had to back over the edge to rappel to get in my growth zone and be victorious. In the four stages of change, we call it the Safety Zone, where you see the risk and go for it.

Lesson four: The Strength of Teamwork

We carried everything we needed for the four-day excursion: food, supplies, and gear. Everyone did their part. When someone was struggling to keep up or fighting fear, amazing words of encouragement were given. There was celebration of accomplishment. We were all stripped of our titles, and we won together. The teamwork was remarkable.

Lesson five: The Simplicity of Life

During those few days, I know I ate less food and burned a ton more calories than back at the office. The norm was to burn fewer calories and eat more food. I was grateful for the hard salami slices, the cheese, and even the bagels, because we were hungry. What we ate was simple. We carried very little food, few clothes; we really didn't need much. We were out there in the wilderness. However, it is true I haven't touched a bagel since I returned.

For those days, it was truly "keep it simple." We needed a lot less than we usually think. Take what you need, but don't carry extra baggage. It was a life-changing experience, as they say, and it shaped my thinking about team performance in ways that I draw on today.

There are five reasons why I think it's important to stop and think about team performance. The first reason, smart people do. Have you ever heard of a guy named Steve Jobs? Well he said, "You've got to be a talent scout because no matter how smart you are, *you need a team* of great people."[42]

Recognizing the reality of today's workplace is the second reason. The workplace can feel like a wilderness or even a battle field. Workplace "wounds" can put teams and careers at risk, even hinder the business in some situations. In today's workplace, the work you do matters, but sometimes it's hard to do what matters because there are so many distractions; we're "so busy." It's easy to lose the vision and the purpose. Success demands a high-performing team. As Anne Sweeney, former president of ABC Television and co-chair of Disney Media Network said, "The number one key to success in every business is the team. It is all about putting together the best team possible."[43]

Another reality of today's workforce is the challenge to manage five generations of workers. Peter Cappelli, professor of management at the Wharton School of Business and coauthor of, *Managing the Older Worker*, writes, "it's more common to see someone younger managing someone older. This can lead to tensions on both sides. Maybe there is a feeling of 'Why am I being bossed around by someone without a lot of experience?' On the other hand, maybe the younger person feels insecure and wonders, 'How do I do this?'"[44]

Writing on generational issues for the *Harvard Business Review*, Rebecca Knight says, "Whether this multigenerational workplace feels happy and productive or challenging and stressful is in large part up to you, the boss. How should you relate to employees of different age groups? How do you motivate someone much younger or much older than you? And finally, what can you do to encourage employees of different generations to share their knowledge?"[45] Frankly, I believe the secret is still: the business of business is people. The goal is to see and respect the people as people, no matter their generation or gender; as people, not cogs in the machine. Creating space in the midst of the chaos, busyness, and distractions will help you see the people.

The third reason why I think it's important to think about team performance is that it's a critical focus of business. Let me ask, what gets in the way of team performance most often? The technical or the relational? Exactly! The business of business is people, so it's the relational. Today's unique work force has four or five generations working together. It's a critical focus of business.

The fourth reason—it's your competitive advantage. As Patrick Lencioni says, "Teamwork remains the one sustainable competitive advantage that has been largely untapped."[46]

The fifth reason to consider team performance is to reap the benefits of self-managed teams. Team behavior matters to the success of your organization. Self-'managed teams build trust, communicate effectively, and accept responsibility for the work. As a result, there is less stress and unnecessary conflict. Such teams are engaged and more fun to work with because they're more productive.

Five Behaviors of a Self-Managed Team

So, if we're going to have a cohesive, self-managed team, what does it take? What are the behaviors of a self-managed team? Patrick Lencioni began the conversation with his best-seller, *The Five Dysfunctions of a Team*. "Like so many other aspects of life, teamwork comes down to mastering a set of behaviors that are at once theoretically uncomplicated, but extremely difficult to put into practice day after day. Success comes only for those groups that overcome the all-too-human behavioral tendencies that corrupt teams and breed dysfunctional politics with them."[47]

I prefer to think of the behaviors as the superglue of teams. A superglued team builds the **foundation of trust**, the first behavior. The team is willing to be vulnerable with each other. They're confident, and they relate with each other in a confidence that their peers' intentions are good. They open up to one another about needing each other. Wiley did a survey and they asked the question: "When coworkers admit their mistakes, do you trust them more?" 84 percent of those responding said, yes. So what does it sound like when there's a vulnerability-based trust? You'll hear, amongst the team, people saying things like, "I'm sorry." "I was wrong." "I need your help." "I'm not sure." "What do you think?" "What am I missing?"[48]

When trust is cultivated, team members give credit where it is due. They're willing to apologize. They learn the work style, the personality styles of others on the team to work together better. They forgive and release grudges. They admit mistakes. They provide information readily. And they squash gossip. I appreciate Simon Sinek's perspective on vulnerability:

> "Being vulnerable doesn't mean we have to crime more or act me. Being vulnerable means admitting we don't know something or that we made a mistake. It's asking for help. The simple expressions make us vulnerable because they leave us open to criticism, humiliation, or attack. If, however, we work in a strong culture, among others around him we feel safe , expressing vulnerability is the most powerful feeling in the world. We feel the love and support from those around us. We open ourselves to learning and growth. And our simple admission invites others to help us . . . that's enhancing our chances for success.
>
> Here's the irony . . . lying, hiding, and faking might make us appear stronger, but it ultimately undermines the culture. The courage to be vulnerable actually makes the organization and all the teams within it, stronger and higher performing."[49]

The second behavior of the self-managed team is they engage in **effective communication**. The dialogue and debate is focused on problem solving, ideas, and concepts, so they avoid making it personal. Their mantra is to ask more, tell less, teach when you can or must. The Wiley survey asked: "Do you think your team would be more effective if people were franker with their opinions?" 71 percent answered, yes. So, with healthy debate and experience, teams experience more productive meetings, they give voice to everyone's ideas, they solve problems, they minimize office politics and gossip, and they address critical topics to move forward.[50]

A **commitment to decisions** is the third behavior for a good team. Clarity around decisions allows a team to move forward with buy in, even while disagreeing on decisions. The Wiley survey inquired: "Do you sometimes feel that team projects suffer because people aren't committed enough?" 86 percent said, yes.[51] What does it sound like when commitment is missing? "I thought we decided to . . ." "When did we decide to do that? I wish we would have discussed this more." "Look, I didn't agree with this decision anyway." But when trust and communication exist, commitment can be secured as the team creates clarity regarding direction. They leave team meetings with an agreement on priorities. They unite around shared objectives and they hone in on and learn from their mistakes.

Team commitment to decisions requires leadership in two ways. The team leader must create space to think and engage in effective communication with all members of the team. Team members must be willing to speak up while in the team meeting, rather than at the water cooler afterward. Commitment means everyone leaves knowing the direction.

The fourth behavior is embrace **personal responsibility**. Accountability or personal responsibility on a self-managed team means there's a willingness to call out peers on performance or behaviors that might hinder the team's success.

The Wiley survey asked the question: "Would your work team be more effective if people were better at holding one another accountable?" An amazing 89 percent of the participants said, yes.[52] When accountability is embraced, the team puts pressure on the "slacker" to improve. The team identifies early warnings regarding potential problems that will affect team victory. Which leads us to the fifth and last behavior.

They **focus on team results**. Team members set aside individual agendas to focus on what is best for the team. The focus is on collective goals, including expectations and outcome-based performance beyond financial measurements alone. The Wiley survey asked the question: "In your work experience, have you seen projects suffer because people put their own needs ahead of the team's needs?" Unfortunately, 87 percent responded, yes.[53] When the focus is on collective results, teams recruit top talent.

There are six benefits of the superglued team. They make better and faster decisions. They tap into the skills and viewpoints of the entire team. They focus on what matters most. They avoid rehashing due to a lack of buy in. They create a competitive advantage, and sixth, they're just more fun to work with.

Wiley Workplace Learning Solutions and Lencioni have partnered to create a team development program and assessment, The Five Behaviors of a Cohesive Team™. To learn more visit www.fivebehaviors.com.

Team Focus Meetings

We've looked at the power of a *personal focus meeting*, you meeting with you, creating space to think to pursue truth in the Story to ensure you are writing the Story you want to tell. I also introduced the value of an *individual focus meeting*, you meeting with your direct reports to connect, create space, and coach to help them write the Stories they want to tell. Now, given all the benefits of developing self-managed teams, we're ready to explore the team *focused meeting* (TFM).

Clarity is the intentional alignment of purpose and structure to achieve victory. Now, let's create clarity around the TFM by answering three questions. Why create space for a TFM? How do you structure a TFM? And what does a TFM win look like?

Why Create Space for a TFM?

You will recall that the outcome of a cohesive team is collective results. What happens in a typical operation? Staff meetings, financial review meetings, even compensation plans are often oriented toward individual performance metrics. It's not unusual to struggle with "turf wars" and a lack of cooperation. According to the *Business Dictionary*, a silo mentality is "a mindset present in some companies when certain departments or sectors do not wish to share information with others at the same company. This type of mentality will reduce the efficiency of the overall operation, reduce morale, and may contribute to the demise of a productive company culture."[54]

As Patrick Lencioni writes, "Silos and the turf wars they enable devastate organizations. They waste resources, kill productivity, and jeopardize the achievement of goals."[55] The intent is not to destroy the structure required to run a business or organization. It is to facilitate the cohesiveness of successful teams at each level with each department working together. Three of the five behaviors of a self-managed team — building trust, personal responsibility (accountability to the team), and focusing on team results—come together in the TFM.

How do you structure a team focused meeting? Basically, the TFM is a consistent (weekly) brief gathering of a team to report in about how they are helping the team win. Think of it as a "stand up meeting," with each member having about five minutes to report in to the team. The basic agenda is called "My Update to the Team," and is provided to guide the meeting. There are three sections to the update.

The first section is an update on the past week's activities. The first questions are as follows: What was the high and low point this past week? How did you influence people? Other questions: What actions did you commit to at our last TFM? What happened? How did it go? What did you learn?

The second section is the update on My Commitment and Focus. The question: What one thing are you focused on (beyond doing the job) that will create value and move the business forward? The expectation is that it is a SMART goal: specific, measurable, attainable, relevant, and time bound. The prompt to help them think about and frame their goals is in this question: from Here to There by when?

Having written a game-changing goal that adds value to the business, the focus turns to behaviors for the third section: How you will get There? What are the observable actions you are in charge of that will help you achieve your next-level goal?

Again, the emphasis of the TFM update is each leader's commitment to the team. Besides your to-do list and tasks of doing the job, what one thing are you focused on that will impact the business for our team?

There's also a utility section on the printed agenda for follow-up notes. This is important because the TFM is primarily creating space to report in to your team. It is allows superglued teams to build trust, communicate, commit, be accountable, and focus on one goal that will deliver results for the team. And, it will be neglected because of busyness and the job, without the discipline of the TFM. Discussion or brainstorming is limited in the TFM. Deeper-dive discussions regarding one department or team are reserved for the individual focus meeting. The notes section is designed to allow the team leader and team member to log important follow-up questions. It's important to the team and the individual that the team leader avoids conducting an IFM or drilling too deeply into an issue in front of the group, both for the sake of time and for the dignity of the other person.

What does the TFM "win" look like? When the team leaves the meeting, focused on doing the right things for the right reasons, that's a win. When the team experiences an effective, efficient, and meaningful investment in one another, that's a win. When the team builds the foundation of trust for a cohesive team by being truthful about progress and failure and the follow through, that's a win. Think about personal responsibility; how many weeks will a manager show up without having fulfilled his or her commitment to the team? When the team success is celebrated, we have a win. And when the team achieves breakthrough performance to get better results, we have won because of a team focused meeting.

We've seen the opportunity for using focus meetings, whether with yourself, your direct reports, or your team, to support communication and accountability to get results. In the next chapter we'll give our attention to the one thing everybody talks about: communication.

CREATE SPACE TO THINK

1. Why do you believe focusing on team performance is important?

2. How cohesive is your team? On a scale of (1) "We don't have this on our team" to (6) "We really get this," how would you rate your team?

   - ☐ Foundation of trust
   - ☐ Effective communication
   - ☐ Commitment to decisions
   - ☐ Embrace personal responsibility
   - ☐ Focus on team results

   Get more resources and templates at
   LeadersCreateSpace.com.

Part Four:

The Secret to Engaging People

Chapter Thirteen

Communication—Two Questions, Four Results

In these troubled, uncertain times, we don't need more command and control. We need better means to engage everyone's intelligence in solving challenges and crises as they arise.

— MARGARET J. WHEATLEY

Becoming a challenger starts with developing an overactive imagination and a serious case of curiosity.

—LIZ WISEMAN.

You don't learn unless you question.

—JOI ITO

Michelle is an emerging leader chosen for the executive leadership program, which includes one-on-one executive coaching. Based on her 360, communication is to be addressed by her personal development plan. Team feedback indicates team members feel manipulated and often minimized by Michelle's approach.

Having spent a few weeks together in one-on-one coaching, it is clear to me she has a "good heart." By that, I mean, she cares about her people, wants to do the right thing, and desires to support both individual and team success. But what her team experiences is her behavior. You could say her behavior betrays her intentions. Her desire is to help her team to succeed, but her approach is having the opposite effect. It is her behavior that betrays her heart.

"Michelle, how do you like being told what to do?" I ask.

"I don't," she replies. "Give me an assignment, set the objectives, and let me go."

"What happens when your boss tells you what to do? How does that affect your relationship with Bobbie?"

"It drives me crazy."

"Why is that?" I continue.

"I really dislike the command-and-control approach. Frankly, when Bobbie tells me what to do and starts that micromanagement crap, I resist. Truthfully, I don't like it and how it affects my performance."

"Well, how do you feel then?" After some hesitation, she continues, "I guess I don't like it because it feels like she's trying to control me *and* the project. Although she talks about delegation, it just feels like she doesn't trust or respect me. Yeah, that's it. I feel minimized."

"How do you think your team feels based on your communication style?"

Silence.

The Communication Mantra

As we discussed, the leadership development Journey takes place when you engage a process of change to expand your personal influence. One essential way you influence others is through trust-building communication. Managers that "tell" minimize their value to the organization and the value of the people on their team. If you are a "teller," instead of one who asks, you're like Google. Google spits out answers by the millions, but the true value of a search is the ability to ask Google the right question. As Pablo Picasso said of calculators and computers, "They are useless. They only give you answers."[56]

There is this myth that if you lead a team or lead an organization, you're supposed to have all the answers. Not only is that an unrealistic expectation, it is self-limiting. This model limits innovation, collaboration, teamwork, and performance improvement. We would be wise to remember Voltaire's recommendation, "Judge a man by his questions rather than his answers."[57] This means we've got to get better at asking. The mantra for next-level leaders is, **"Ask more, tell less, teach when you can or must."** (Note: the focus of the mantra does not include setting of expectations or giving of instructions. "Ask more" guides you when you desire to create space for another to think or you wish to engage someone in effective communication.)

Why Is It Hard to Stop Telling?

I find there are four common reasons why managers practice this unproductive behavior of telling. The first is *habit*. Telling is your historical approach, and you believe it works. It got you Here, right? The second reason is *speed*. Why go to all that effort to ask questions? Just cut to the chase, tell them what to do; it's faster. Experience and knowledge are part of being a manager. The third reason you may tell is that you already *know the answers*, so why ask, just direct them. The fourth reason to tell involves your *emotions*. When frustrated, it's easy to lose self-control, so you just tell them how it's going to be. You're the manager and have authority. "Because I said so; I'm the boss, and I'm right."

As Peter Drucker correctly states, "My greatest strength as a consultant is to be ignorant and ask a few questions."[58] Substitute "manager" or "leader" for "consultant" in Drucker's statement, and you're hearing truth in the Story.

Two Questions to Guide Your Approach

Imagine you need to engage someone in a conversation about an issue at work. It's a direct report or team member or someone in another department. As you prepare for the conversation, the first question for you to answer is, "What do I want in this situation, control or influence?"

People of influence know they're *in-charge* but **not** in control. Control is an illusion. What happens when you try to control someone or something that is beyond your control? If there is anything at stake, any emotion, challenge, resistance, then most likely you'll lose control, your self-control. Much of the unproductive behavior in relationships comes from either unfulfilled expectations or trying to control another person or situation. When you think about it, you know you cannot control people or things in life. All we can control is ourselves and that can be hard work. Think of a parent-child or spouse relationship. How well do your efforts to control that person work?

COMMUNICATION: TWO QUESTIONS, FOUR RESULTS

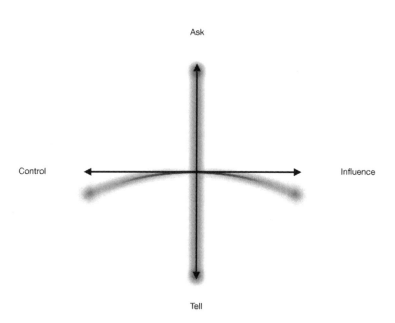

One of your leadership objectives is to create space to think, first for yourself, then for others. Ask yourself this question: "What do I want in the situation, control or influence?" The second question to help you prepare your approach to this conversation is, "How will I begin? Will I need to ask or tell?"

Four Results Based on Your Approach

How you answer these two questions—(1) What do I want, control or influence? (2) What's my approach, ask or tell?—will lead to four different results in your communication.

In Quadrant I, when you come from a place of trying to control and asking, the person will likely feel manipulated. Here, you seek to cleverly control the conversation. Think about the courtroom and listen for the leading question. "On the night of September 4th, isn't it true that you were at the corner of . . . " The other type of question used in Quadrant I is a closed question, to which the desired answers are limited to yes or no. Both leading and closed questions speed up the exchange. When you're in an emotionally charged situation with pride and/or fear activated, it's the perfect setup for a heated exchange or a silent surrender, otherwise known as the fight-or-flight response.

In Quadrant II, you'll see what happens when you come from a place of control while telling. The goal of this approach is control. The words are declarative or emphatic and can be delivered with a forceful tone, "This is what you're going to do." Notice how if you start with a desire to control, the left side of the quadrant, your communication will likely leave the other person feeling manipulated or dominated. How productive is that?

To engage someone, work in Quadrant III; here the key word is **think**. Your motive is to influence (not control) the other person, and your method is to ask open-ended questions. Yes, you're in charge, but with nothing to prove. Your desire is to engage the other person. Your goal is to create space for the other person to think, and avoid pushing them into a fight-or-flight mode. Instead, they're invited to stay and to engage with you in the conversation. You use open-ended questions. We'll talk more about that in a moment.

Now, we're at Quadrant IV, where the keyword is **learn**. Learning occurs when you come from a place of influence and telling becomes teaching. Having demonstrated interest in the other person by asking open-ended questions, you have prepared them to learn as they discover the limits of their knowledge. You have connected, showed respect with your approach, and they are now prepared to learn. This is possible as you appeal to their desire to learn and to grow, rather than being told. They're ready to gain knowledge or skill by being taught something new.

COMMUNICATION: TWO QUESTIONS, FOUR RESULTS

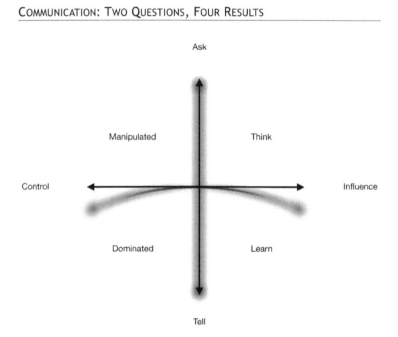

As Joi Ito, says, ""If the learner is doing the questioning, it's very different from when an examiner (or teacher) is doing the questioning. When you have the examiner doing the questioning, you're in what I would call education mode. I think education is something other people do to you, whereas learning is what you do to yourself."[59] Telling is converted to teaching. Receptivity is cultivated, and your approach makes learning possible in Quadrant II. As the folks at the Right Question Institute say, "Questioning is the ability to organize our thinking around what we don't know."[60] Congratulations, you've created space for someone to step into their growth zone and learn. You've engaged them by demonstrating respect and valuing their input.

How to Frame Questions to Engage Others

As someone pointed out, "Knowing the answers will help you in school, knowing how to question will help you in life." Here are two suggestions to help you effectively engage others.

Although it's sometimes difficult, the first thing to do is release the need or urge to control. Yes, you're in charge of the work or the department, but not in control.

Next, be curious. The leader in the room asks questions, versus having all the answers. "It's a miracle that curiosity survives formal education," Albert Einstein once said.[61] How deep is your desire to investigate? What has happened to your desire to learn and to know? What were you like when you were a kid?

Researchers at the University of Michigan explored why young children ask so many why questions. They concluded that, "Curiosity plays a big part in preschoolers' lives . . . Children are motivated by a desire for explanation." The researchers found that when children "got answers that weren't explanations, they seemed dissatisfied and were more likely to repeat their original question or provide an alternative explanation. When they asked Why questions, they were trying to get to the bottom of things."[62]

Author and technology executive Sheryl Sandberg knows the importance of curiosity when she writes, "A powerful tribute to the ways innovation and disruptive thinking stem from a common trait: curiosity. The little girl who asks 'Why is the sky blue?' becomes a woman who can change the world."[63] If you can't remember what it was like when you were a kid, spend some time with children under the age of six, and hear their curiosity.

Anchor Your Question

To frame an effective question, anchor it. Like a heavy object attached to a chain on a large ship holds the vessel in place, the first word of your question helps you stay on point. There are three steps to an engaging conversation. Release your need to control. Cultivate your curiosity.

Anchor your question. To frame an open-ended question, the anchor word is the strongest and most important part. It's the first word of the question. Here are some classic anchor words to help get you started.

- **Who**—when the question relates to the people to be involved or who's responsible. *Who will this decision affect? Who will take care of the contract?*
- **What**—"what" is the great, general-discovery anchor word. For example, *What am I missing?*
- **When**—speaks to a time-related answer. *When would we need to start, to meet the deadline? When will the project be completed?*
- **Where**—speaks of place and location. For example, *Where would we move the department, if we go with this plan?*
- **Why**—seeks clarity regarding purpose or motive. It leads to a deeper dive into a situation. If used to dig deeper into someone's action, you must watch your tone and nonverbal communication. If you anchor with "Why" regarding a performance issue, it's easy to sound accusatory. The tone of voice is always important with the use of the word, why. *Why do we think that happened?*
- **How**—the solid anchor used to connect the dots. *How would that work? How many customers will that affect? How would we handle this transition?*
- **What if**—when you want to float an idea, keep "What if" at the ready. *What if we postpone the purchase until next quarter? What if you lead this discussion in the board retreat? The idea is to provide input without commanding it.*

By the way, the phrase "tell me more" is not an anchor for an open-ended question. One last tip, watch your pronoun selection. Avoid the singular pronoun "you" in your question, and use the plural pronoun "we" instead. It helps put you and the person whom you want to engage in effective dialogue on the same side of the table.

The Benefits of Asking

If your desire is to expand your influence with people through more effective communication, then commit to *ask more and tell less*. As American novelist and short story writer Richard Ford says, "When people realize they're being listened to, they tell you things."[64] There are at least four relationship benefits associated with the well-framed question. The first is honor. When you seek another person's input, they feel respected and valued; they feel honored. Second, a well-timed question slows down the conversation. It creates space in a positive way, so that objectivity can be gained over an emotional reaction.

Third, cooperation. Supported decisions and a willingness to commit are more likely to be achieved when we engage others with well-framed questions. The fourth relationship benefit is improved performance. When people feel respected, feel their voice has been heard, and gain objectivity, it leads to trust, commitment, and better results.

Notice the difference when you ask, "What are your thoughts on this plan?" instead of, "I've been thinking about this, and here is what you're going to do." What moves you to action? What inspires you? What engages you?

Ask more, tell less, teach when you can or must.

Stay Engaged Longer

If there's a secret to expanding your influence with people, it's the skill of framing and asking open-ended questions to create space to think and learn. Surely, it's obvious how few people want to feel dominated or manipulated in a conversation, a planning session, or team meeting. It will require determination. It will take time for people in your life to believe you really want to know what they think, to get used to being asked to give their perspective and creative insight. I mean, they're used to being told, right? (Yes, that is a leading question.) It will also require determination because "people don't think," and you'll be creating space to think. You'll be asking them to think. Embrace the silence and the need to process when necessary.

A word of caution. As you develop the discipline and habit of asking more, watch that you don't "machine gun" the other person with rapid-fire questions, without giving them time to answer.

For many people, the first response is to deflect the question. Be prepared to hear responses such as, "Oh, I don't know; I'm not sure." When it's an emotionally charged and difficult conversation, you may hear, "How should I know?" with a bit of defensiveness. Here you must be disciplined not to take the bait and move back into telling, your comfort zone.

A couple of suggestions to help you during this transition when your questions are being deflected. First, acknowledge their response by saying something like, "I hear you," and then, repeat the question. Or, you can respond with, "I see"; then, repeat the question.

Albert Einstein modeled this approach when he said, "It's not that I'm so smart, but that I stay with the questions much longer." You will, in fact, have to stay with the questions, as you shift from telling to asking.

Be Prepared

As you embrace the mantra—ask more, tell less, teach when you can or must—you may find it necessary and helpful to prepare yourself. Here's a short checklist to help you think about the conversation that you want to prepare for.

The first matter to assess is *what are your current assumptions, opinions, judgments, or conclusions?* What are you accepting as true, without verification? What's your bias? Second, *what do you want to happen in this conversation and situation?* Third, *what do you want for the other person, for your relationship with the other person, and for the business itself?* And last on the checklist, *how will you create space to think? What questions will you ask?* Write them down before the meeting. There's nothing wrong with having a sheet of questions for your review. Then, if necessary, how will you create space to learn? As a mentor or teacher, what questions could you have ready to ask to help them connect the dots? Remember, open-ended questions are still in your toolbox, even when you're in teaching mode.

If there is a secret to influence, it's more effective communication. Here are three suggestions I'll leave you with. Stop talking. Release the need to control. Be curious; cultivate your curiosity. As Walt Disney revealed, his secret is, "We keep moving forward, opening new doors and doing new things, because we're curious and curiosity keeps leading us down new paths."[65]

The business of business is people, right? People want to be lead or influenced, not managed, but coached. Before we conclude our conversation, explore the following questions about your communication.

CREATE SPACE TO THINK

1. How would you describe your communication approach?
2. Why is it easier to tell than ask open-ended questions?
3. What would happen if you stopped talking?

Chapter Fourteen

The Business of Business Is People, So What?

A good coach can change a game. A great coach can change a life.
—John Wooden

The wheel, look around and you see them everywhere. Compared to a "smartphone," we may rush to judgment at how primitive the invention is. According to Ancient-Origins' website: *"The wheel (specifically as a means of transportation) was actually invented at a relatively late point of human history. The oldest known wheel found in an archaeological excavation is from Mesopotamia, and dates to around 3500 BC. By this time, human beings were already planting crops, herding domesticated animals, and had some form of social hierarchy."*[66]

It's likely that the first use of a wheel was not for transportation, but was used by potters 5500 years ago. It was some 300 years later that the wheel began its story.

It appears that man first used the wheel to speed up his pottery job. Next, he experimented with transportation by connecting two wheels to a rustic axle, creating a cart to move stuff easier, faster, further. It was good enough, for a while. Then, someone connected the wagon and the power of a horse to create the horse-drawn wagon and in short order, the carriage to move people. The stagecoach passenger enjoyed protection from the elements and an accelerated journey, as they jiggled forward.

In 1823, the first steam locomotive carried passengers on a public rail. Privileged passengers experienced the significant improvement of the railroad. The seat on a train once again provided eager travelers the ability to go further and faster on their journeys.

Today, you could drive from Los Angeles to New York in forty-two hours and travel less than five hours by jet airplane. Now, we can travel further and faster. We've come a long way, in a short time, from the stage coach. While there's no need to speed up the pace of life, what if we could accelerate the growth and development of today's workforce? How can you, as leader, coach your team to move further, faster—from Here to There? The challenge is that when it comes to leadership development you must slow down to accelerate, which means you will create space to think, create clarity to act, and create opportunities to get better. It is the Here-to-There Journey, and it helps to have support.

Where Are You Taking Us, Coach?

Coaches instruct or train players in a sport, fine arts, business, career, financial, health and wellness, education, life, and relationships. Coaches move people further and faster. We probably best understand and observe coaching in individual and team sports. However, in recent years, the value of leadership coaching has become more accepted as part of human resource development for business leaders. As a coach, I help teams and leaders make their next-level journey from Here to There, at an accelerated pace by slowing down. What if you embrace a coaching relationship with your team? How could that affect performance?

Since you're reading this book, you believe leadership development is important to you, your team, and your business. The question is not "Will you take the next-level journey?"—you're already committed. What's up for grabs is how you will accelerate the trip. How long will it take to get from Here to There? How much pain must be endured to get you out of your comfort zone and into the growth zone, and how will you get your team there with you?

Clearly, there's no need to increase the pace of life. If you desire greater success, if you recognize the need for leadership development, if you want to expand your influence with talented people, if you desire to help others achieve their full potential, you must embrace the counterintuitive practice of slowing down to speed up the Journey. The coaching manager is a leader who creates space to think, creates clarity to act, and creates the opportunity to get better and to produce breakthrough performance. Coaching is the accelerator.

Managers who understand this not only embrace coaching for themselves, but create a culture of coaching. They stop talking and listen. They ask more and tell less. They become more mindful and emotionally intelligent. They set clear expectations. They build trust, engage others in open dialogue, secure buy in and commitment, hold their team accountable, and produce team results. They slow down to accelerate the Here-to-There Journey. The coaching leader believes personal growth, professional development, and results can be accelerated when you create space.

Three Functions of the Coaching Leader

As a coach, you are responsible to cultivate an environment and a culture that inspires people. It is to build trust, to engage in effective communication, to secure commitment, to encourage personal responsibility, and focus on collective results. These five behaviors are the superglue of team performance. Leaders who take this approach will find themselves developing far more effective teams. That's because coaches change people's lives, even if it's simply the difference in their attitude at the start of the day.

Great coaches connect to show team members their potential, help them gain confidence in their work, and point out the value of what they do, while inspiring them to be the best they can be. Remember the three functions of the coaching manager discussed in chapter three, as you pursue this role. Your first function is to connect, to *recruit your team*. As Jim Collins writes, "Those who build great organizations make sure they have the right people on the bus and the right people in the key seats before they figure out where to drive the bus. They always think first about who and then about what. When facing chaos and uncertainty, and you cannot possibly predict what's coming around the corner, your best "strategy" is to have a busload of people who can adapt to and perform brilliantly no matter what comes next. Great vision without great people is irrelevant."[67] The approach is to *connect* to discover the Story. The question to ask is "How did we get Here?"

Coaches also *create space.* They help people think and create clarity to avoid confusion. The approach is to explore the possibilities. The question to ask is "What does There look like?"

The third function is to *coach.* You see the person, choose to serve, and care about the person. The question to ask, "How can we get There?"

What do people think about coaches who connect, create, and coach? Consider what Pro Football Hall of Fame member and former NFL coach Mike Singletary says, "Players respond to coaches who really had their best interest at heart." Makes sense, right?[68]

The Power of Story

Your goal as a coaching leader is to help someone get from Here to There in their career and Journey, and to help them write the Story they want to tell. As Bill McCartney correctly points out, "All coaching is, is taking a player where he can't take himself."[69] Here are some additional tips to help you be a coaching leader. Schedule regular individual focus meetings with each member of your team. This requires the dedication and prioritization of your calendar. Investing in your team's life matters. We develop trust and relationships through time spent together. Becoming like-minded is a by-product of helping your leadership team learn to think the way you think. The consistent individual focus meeting is designed to support this commitment.

To serve others as a coaching leader also requires your commitment to seek truth in the Story. By truth, I mean get the facts—what's really going on? what really happened? Truth includes feedback, experience, success, and failure. "What's the truth in the Story?" is a great question and is easier to ask when relationships are healthy. As a coach, part of your role is to help people connect the dots, to recognize their unproductive behaviors that will hold them back from future success. To create an opportunity to get better.

The IFM allows you to manage expectations and provide specific and timely feedback. It is a coaching opportunity focused on both leadership and business development. You can help individuals transform the disruption by creating space to think and creating clarity for their lives and for the business. As a leader committed to growth, you will engage them in a process of change to expand their personal influence.

To be an effective coaching leader is to use the three creative disciplines. The first is to create space to think, which is the disciplined use of time, place, and resources to reflect on truth in the Story. The second discipline is to create clarity to act, to deliberately align purpose and structure to achieve victory. And the third discipline is to create the opportunity to get better. To experience breakthrough performance, bust through opposition, hindrances, and unproductive behaviors to get results and achieve success requires inspired people doing inspired work.

As you move into the role of coaching leader, remember the five realities of the Story. Everyone has a Story. Every day we add to the Story. There's always more to the Story. Today, you will influence someone else's Story. You're responsible to write your Story and help others write the Story they want to tell in life.

If There's a Silver Bullet

If there's a silver bullet, it is to embrace the freedom of letting go. When we seek to change behavior and build new habits, we may have to relax into it. Once you catch the vision and see the promise of There, you may become impatient with yourself or others. Relax into it. Let the process of change work.

Release your propensity to control and instead, seek influence as the one in charge. Release your grip on being "the expert" and recapture your childlike curiosity. Stop talking and become an active listener; monitor how much of the conversation you dominate. As an active listener, pay attention, and be disciplined to listen without forming your response while the other person is speaking. Give your undivided attention, make eye contact, uncross your arms, silence the "stupid" smartphone, minimize distractions, treat the IFM as sacred time. Pay attention, and you'll be paid back in full.

Leaders create space, remembering the mantra, *ask more, tell less, teach when you can or must.* The silver bullet is in the mantra. When you take care of your people, your people will take care of the business, and together, you will transform disruption into clarity for life and business.

CREATE SPACE TO THINK

1. What's your plan to accelerate your development? Your team's?

2. Who are you coaching? Who is your coach helping you go further than you can go by yourself?

3. Who are the people of influence in your life?

My Gratitude

On Thursday morning, February 8, 2018, I sent a text message to my family, some clients, and a few colleagues. *"I just hit 'Send' to submit my manuscript for Leaders Create Space. Exhale. Nervous. Hopeful. Thanks for your contribution to my Journey and this work."* One of my clients tactfully responded, *"Hope you are able to throw the word "celebrate" in there somewhere!"*

So I come to celebrate.

This book, like anything of value, is created out of a lifetime of stories. To connect all the dots is impossible. Who nudged me to take action, to believe, to create, to think, and speak? Which conversation, which sentence from another's writing delivered another "ahha moment?" Who unknowingly provided timely affirmation and encouragement to keep going? Whose story produced a moment of insight and understanding? Thank you to the women and men brave enough to let me in on their journey, who trusted me with their story of pain and promise, success and failure, and that drive to become a better leader.

Yes, I am grateful.

Thanks to Rob Kosberg and the team at Best Sellers Publishing. Randy Taylor - the way you embraced the message was impressive, thanks for your commitment. To Rebecca Grosch for getting things moving. And, Burke Mohan - thanks for engaging the content beyond your work as an editor and Sydney Hubbard for shepherding the process. To everyone who worked behind the scenes, thank you. So much encouragement, openness, and support for the long road of creative work.

Thank you to the researchers and writers who shared their work. As Seth Godin correctly points out, "One can't write without using the ideas, metaphors, styles, tropes, processes, concepts, examples and successes that came before. The writing would be incoherent, it wouldn't resonate with anyone and failure would ensue." (The quote is from his blog post, "Stolen ideas.") So to all who came before me, your discoveries provided me insight and increased my understanding. Richard Boyatzis, Anne McKee, Henry Cloud, Patrick Lencioni, The Arbinger Institute, Simon Sinek, Bernadette Jiwa, John Maxwell, Jim Loehr, Tony Schwartz, Travis Bradberry, Seth Godin, Marshall Goldsmith, Marcus Buckingham, Darren Hardy to name a few.

To my colleague, Pam Cho for all our "Mojo Monday" calls and how you are such an encourager. To Brigette Steinheider for bringing confirmation to the Next Level Coaching process from an international, academic, and personal perspective. For your modeling of team-based learning that helped shape NLEC's team-based coaching. Thank you for introducing me to so many outstanding students in your Organizational Dynamics (ODYN) Master of Arts program. To Todd Craig for trusting me first as your coach and then, for time, energy, and enthusiasm you contributed to this writing journey, this book is only better because of you. And Stephanie Isbell, I'll never forget how Google connected our paths, how committed you are to transformation and receptive to our conversations. I learned a lot from you. You contributed so much to this book with your wisdom, understanding, and professional expertise.

To David Litzinger and his leadership team (Tim, John, and Doug) thank you for the privilege of joining you in the pursuit of making business about the people, being recognized as a leader in your industry, with a commitment to get better every day. What an honor to serve as your "partner." To all my coaching clients, it is humbling to receive your trust, transparency, and to experience your breakthroughs. Please know how much I learned from you.

To my parents, Jim and Vivian, for your support and my faith-based heritage. To my best friend and my life-long love for over 42 years, thank you, Rita, for the encouragement to go for it. I don't know what I'd do without you. To our daughters Stephanie, Monica, and Melanie I believe in you, relax into the process, but keep pushing into your potential. To our ten grandchildren, I pray for each of you, that you will learn to lead your life and write the story you will want to tell.

To my Lord and Savior Jesus Christ, thank you for the ongoing transformation of my life and for the calling to do this work. What an amazing second half.

Notes and References

Chapter 2

1. https://hbr.org/2016/12/research-why-americans-are-so-impressed-by-busyness "Why Americans Are So Impressed by Busyness," Harvard Business Review, December 15, 2016

2. Hunch, Bernadette Jiwa, Page 34 Portfolio/Penguin Copyright 2017

3. They Can't Eat You, Marc Sparks, page 158

4. https://www.brainyquote.com/quotes/henry_david_thoreau_153926

5. https://hbr.org/2011/04/failure-chronicles

6. https://hbr.org/2012/09/ten-reasons-people-resist-chang

Chapter 3

7. http://www.overviewinstitute.org/about-us/declaration-of-vision-and-principles

8. "Overview," Planetary Collection video https://vimeo.com/55073825

9. "Overview," Planetary Collection video https://vimeo.com/55073825

10. The Son, Ch. 4, p. 45 - Report to Greco (1965) http://izquotes.com/quote/242853

11. Resonant Leadership, Richard Boyatzis and Annie McKee, Harvard Business School Press, Chapter 1, Page 3

12. Oh, the Places You'll Go!, Dr. Seuss

Chapter 4

13. https://www.britannica.com/place/Mount-Everest

14. "From Comfort Zone to Performance Management," Alasdair White, White & Maclean Publishing, 2008, p. 2, http://www.whiteandmaclean.eu/uploaded_files/120120109110852performance_management-final290110(2)-preview.pdf

Chapter 5

15. Thinking for a Change, John C. Maxwell, Pages 27-33

Chapter 6

16. "T.D. Jakes Wants You to Suffer" Amy Anderson, Success. July 2017, p 42

17. Resonant Leadership, Richard Boyatzis and Annie McKee, Harvard Business School Press, p. 9

18. How to Have That Difficult Conversation You've Been Avoiding, Henry Cloud and John Townsend, p. 20

19. Crucial Conversations, Patterson, Grenny, McMillan, and Switzler

Chapter 7

20. http://blog.teachersource.com/2014/01/18/chemistry-of-tarnished-silver/

Chapter 8

21. Gallup Report 2017, State of the American Workplace, P. 5

22. Gallup Report 2017, State of the American Workplace, P.190

23. Gallup Report 2017, State of the American Workplace, P.63. For more information on the Q12 Survey go to https://q12.gallup.com.

24. Gallup Report 2017, State of the American Workplace, P.63

25. Gallup Report 2017, State of the American Workplace, P.63

26. drcloud.com "The 3 Step Recipe for Making Really Successful People." https://drcloud.com/article/The_3_Step_Recipe_for_Making_Really_Successful_People?utm_source=Daily+Dr+Cloud&utm_campaign=5491346a9f-EMAIL_CAMPAIGN_2017_02_11&utm_medium=email&utm_term=0_b577372d86-5491346a9f-7462993&mc_cid=5491346a9f&mc_eid=b42f7d30b1

Chapter 9

27. http://www.nytimes.com/2011/03/13/business/13hire.html

28. "Google's Quest to Build a Better Boss," Adam Bryant, The New York Times, March 12, 2011. http://www.nytimes.com/2011/03/13/business/13hire.html?pagewanted=1&_r=1&ref=business&src=me

29. http://www.businessinsider.com/8-habits-of-highly-effective-google-managers-2011-3

30. http://www.margaretwheatley.com/articles/howisyourleadership.html

Chapter 10

31. http://journals.sagepub.com/doi/abs/10.1177/0956797614524581

32. https://www.scientificamerican.com/article/a-learning-secret-don-t-take-notes-with-a-laptop/#

33. http://www.ushistory.org/franklin/autobiography/page37.htm

Chapter 11

34. https://www.success.com/article/simon-sinek-the-secret-to-leadership-and-millennials-is-simply-purpose

35. *The Power of the Other,* Henry Cloud, p. 176

36. https://www.success.com/article/john-c-maxwell-why-you-need-to-surround-yourself-with-like-valued-people

37. http://www.nytimes.com/2011/03/13/business/13hire.html

38. First, Break All the Rules, Marcus Buckingham and Curt Coffman, p. 28

39. http://www.success.com/blog/the-often-overlooked-ingredient-for-winning-at-life

40. https://www.forbes.com/sites/jefffromm/2015/11/06/millennials-in-the-workplace-they-dont-need-trophies-but-they-want-reinforcement/#4203a3df53f6

41. *The Power of the Other,* Henry Cloud, p. 157

Chapter 12

42. https://www.cnbc.com/2017/11/15/steve-jobs-bill-gates-how-to-be-successful.html?view=story&%24DEVICE%24=native-android-mobile

43. https://www.success.com/article/from-the-corner-office-disney-abc-president-anne-sweeney

44. https://hbr.org/2014/09/managing-people-from-5-generations

45. https://hbr.org/2014/09/managing-people-from-5-generations

46. The Five Dysfunctions of a Team, Patrick Lencioni

47. The Five Dysfunctions of a Team, Patrick Lencioni P. viii

48. The Five Behaviors of a Cohesive Team, Facilitator's Guide, by John Wiley & Sons, Inc. Page 6-7

49. Together is Better by Simon Sinek, page 134

50. The Five Behaviors of a Cohesive Team, Facilitator's Guide, by John Wiley & Sons, Inc. Page 8

51. The Five Behaviors of a Cohesive Team, Facilitator's Guide, by John Wiley & Sons, Inc. Page 9

52. The Five Behaviors of a Cohesive Team, Facilitator's Guide, by John Wiley & Sons, Inc. Page 9

53. The Five Behaviors of a Cohesive Team, Facilitator's Guide, by John Wiley & Sons, Inc. Page 10

54. http://www.businessdictionary.com/definition/silo-mentality.html

55. The Five Dysfunctions of a Team, Patrick Lencioni

Chapter 13

56. https://quoteinvestigator.com/2011/11/05/computers-useless/

57. https://www.bookbrowse.com/quotes/detail/index.cfm/quote_number/406/judge-a-man-by-his-questions-rather-than-by-his-answers

58. http://www.druckerinstitute.com/2014/03/asking-the-right-questions/

59. http://amorebeautifulquestion.com/today-cant-afford-become-adults/

60. A More Beautiful Question, Warren Berger, p. 19

61. https://www.scribd.com/document/141870649/Curiosity-Survives-Formal-Education

62. https://www.sciencedaily.com/releases/2009/11/091113083254.htm

63. https://www.leadershipnow.com/leadershop/9781476730752.html

64. http://tumblr.austinkleon.com/post/23424640934

65. https://www.brainyquote.com/quotes/walt_disney_132637

Chapter 14

66. http://www.ancient-origins.net/ancient-technology/revolutionary-invention-wheel-001713

67. http://www.jimcollins.com/concepts/first-who-then-what.html

68. http://www.espn.com/nfl/news/story?id=3675428

69. https://www.brainyquote.com/quotes/bill_mccartney_381122

About the Author

With a passion for helping people reach their full potential, Steve Laswell is one of the most effective certified executive coaches in America. Steve is the author of two other books *The People Project: Your Guide for Changing Behavior and Growing Your Influence as a Leader and The Journey: Personal Notes from The Father.* In addition to his work as an author, Steve speaks to people on topics relating to leadership and personal development, teams, and organizational development. He loves to connect with people, create opportunities to think, learn, and change he cares about people. Steve creates a supportive and safe relationship where his clients are free to pursue truth in the Story to change behavior and expand influence. Real and profound change occurs in relationships built on the foundation of trust.

Steve is also the founder and president of Next Level Executive Coaching, LLC a coaching practice committed to executive and team-based coaching designed to develop self-managed teams and leaders. Next Level Partners, his clients, take advantage of the following professional services:

- One-on-One Executive Coaching
- Team-based Coaching
- Organizational Development Coaching
- Speaking Services

He received a master's degree from Southern Nazarene University and his bachelor's degree from Mid-American Nazarene University. He served in the faith-based, non-profit sector for nearly 20 years before his fast-track radio career. In ten years, he went from being a rookie account manager with Clear Channel Communications - OKC to

Station Manager of Cox Radio's five-station cluster in Tulsa, Oklahoma. He launched Next Level Executive Coaching in January 2008.

Steve lives in Tulsa, Oklahoma with Rita, his wife of 42 years. They have three daughters and ten grandchildren. To learn more about Steve and Next Level Executive Coaching, please visit:

www.nextlevelexecutivecoaching.com.
If you'd like to connect with Steve directly,
you can reach him at **918-630-9761** or
steve@nextlevelexecutivecoaching.com.

Get more resources and templates at
LeadersCreateSpace.com.